Hydropower Efficiency, Grade 4

What if you could challenge your fourth graders to create a minimally invasive, highly efficient dam? With this volume in the *STEM Road Map Curriculum Series*, you can! *Hydropower Efficiency* outlines a journey that will steer your students toward authentic problem solving while grounding them in integrated STEM disciplines. Like the other volumes in the series, this book is designed to meet the growing need to infuse real-world learning into K–12 classrooms.

This interdisciplinary, four-lesson module uses project- and problem-based learning to help students create a highly efficient dam that has a minimal impact on the environment. Students will explore the use of natural resources to provide energy needs, specifically hydropower, while exploring the workings of watermills, wind turbines, and generators to help build an understanding of the effects of dams. In creating their dam, they will learn about the various types of alternative hydropower sources, including wave and tidal power, and track the progress of electrification in the U.S. on a timeline; alongside researching the positive and negative consequences of hydropower.

To support this goal, students will do the following:

- Use the engineering design process (EDP) to create a design for a dam, wind turbine, and water wheel

- Compare and contrast renewable power sources

- Evaluate power sources for efficiency

- Identify positive and negative consequences of human modifications of the environment

- Identify and describe how several sources of renewable energy are used across the U.S.

- Use mapping skills to determine where natural resources are being accessed for energy usage

- Effectively utilize shapes, materials, and measurements to create a model of a hydropower system.

The *STEM Road Map Curriculum Series* is anchored in the Next Generation Science Standards, the Common Core State Standards, and the Framework for 21st Century Learning. In-depth and flexible, *Hydropower Efficiency* can be used as a whole unit or in part to meet the needs of districts, schools, and teachers who are charting a course toward an integrated STEM approach.

Carla C. Johnson is a Professor of Science Education and Office of Research and Innovation Faculty Research Fellow at North Carolina State University, North Carolina, USA.

Janet B. Walton is a Senior Research Scholar at North Carolina State University's College of Education in Raleigh, North Carolina, USA.

Erin E. Peters-Burton is the Donna R. and David E. Sterling Endowed Professor in Science Education at George Mason University in Fairfax, Virginia, USA.

THE STEM ROAD MAP CURRICULUM SERIES

Series editors: Carla C. Johnson, Janet B. Walton, and Erin E. Peters-Burton

Map out a journey that will steer your students toward authentic problem solving as you ground them in integrated STEM disciplines.

Co-published by Routledge and NSTA Press, in partnership with the National Science Teaching Association, this K–12 curriculum series is anchored in the Next Generation Science Standards, the Common Core State Standards, and the Framework for 21st Century Learning. It was developed to meet the growing need to infuse real-world STEM learning into classrooms.

Each book is an in-depth module that uses project- and problem-based learning. First, your students are presented with a challenge. Then, they apply what they learn using science, social studies, English language arts, and mathematics. Engaging and flexible, each volume can be used as a whole unit or in part to meet the needs of districts, schools, and teachers who are charting a course toward an integrated STEM approach.

Modules are available from NSTA Press and Routledge, and organized under the following themes. For an update listing of the volumes in the series, please visit https://www.routledge.com/STEM-Road-Map-Curriculum-Series/book-series/SRM (for titles co-published by Routledge and NSTA Press), or www.nsta.org/book-series/stem-road-map-curriculum (for titles published by NSTA Press).

Co-published by Routledge and NSTA Press:

Optimizing the Human Experience:

- *Our Changing Environment, Grade K: STEM Road Map for Elementary School*
- *Genetically Modified Organisms, Grade 7: STEM Road Map for Middle School*
- *Rebuilding the Natural Environment, Grade 10: STEM Road Map for High School*
- *Mineral Resources, Grade 11: STEM Road Map for High School*

Cause and Effect:

- *Formation of the Earth, Grade 9: STEM Road Map for High School*

Sustainable Systems:

- *Habitats in the United States, Grade K: STEM Road Map for Elementary School*
- *Habitats Local and Far Away, Grade 1: STEM Road Map for Elementary School*
- *Hydropower Efficiency, Grade 4: STEM Road Map for Elementary School*
- *Composting, Grade 5: STEM Road Map for Elementary School*
- *Global Population Issues, Grade 7: STEM Road Map for Middle School*
- *The Speed of Green, Grade 8: STEM Road Map for Middle School*
- *Creating Global Bonds, Grade 12: STEM Road Map for High School*

Published by NSTA Press:

Innovation and Progress:

- *Amusement Park of the Future, Grade 6: STEM Road Map for Elementary School*
- *Transportation in the Future, Grade 3: STEM Road Map for Elementary School*

- *Harnessing Solar Energy, Grade 4: STEM Road Map for Elementary School*
- *Wind Energy, Grade 5: STEM Road Map for Elementary School*
- *Construction Materials, Grade 11: STEM Road Map for High School*

The Represented World:

- *Patterns and the Plant World, Grade 1: STEM Road Map for Elementary School*
- *Investigating Environmental Changes, Grade 2: STEM Road Map for Elementary School*
- *Swing Set Makeover, Grade 3: STEM Road Map for Elementary School*
- *Rainwater Analysis, Grade 5: STEM Road Map for Elementary School*
- *Packaging Design, Grade 6: STEM Road Map for Middle School*
- *Improving Bridge Design, Grade 8: STEM Road Map for Middle School*
- *Radioactivity, Grade 11: STEM Road Map for High School*
- *Car Crashes, Grade 12: STEM Road Map for High School*

Cause and Effect:

- *Physics in Motion, Grade K: STEM Road Map for Elementary School*
- *Influence of Waves, Grade 1: STEM Road Map for Elementary School*
- *Natural Hazards, Grade 2: STEM Road Map for Elementary School*
- *Human Impacts on Our Climate, Grade 6: STEM Road Map for Middle School*
- *The Changing Earth, Grade 8: STEM Road Map for Middle School*
- *Healthy Living, Grade 10: STEM Road Map for High School*

Hydropower Efficiency

Grade
4

STEM Road Map for Elementary School

Edited by Carla C. Johnson, Janet B. Walton, and
Erin E. Peters-Burton

Routledge
Taylor & Francis Group
NEW YORK AND LONDON

nsta Press
National Science Teaching Association

Designed cover image: © Shutterstock

First published 2024
by Routledge
605 Third Avenue, New York, NY 10158

and by Routledge
4 Park Square, Milton Park, Abingdon, Oxon, OX14 4RN

Routledge is an imprint of the Taylor & Francis Group, an informa business

A co-publication with NSTA Press

ISBN: 978-1-032-61814-2 (hbk)
ISBN: 978-1-032-61807-4 (pbk)
ISBN: 978-1-032-61819-7 (ebk)

DOI: 10.4324/9781032618197

Typeset in PalatinoLTStd
by MPS Limited, Dehradun

Access the support material: www.routledge.com/9781032618142

CONTENTS

CONTENTS

Part 2: Hydropower Efficiency: STEM Road Map Module

CONTENTS

ABOUT THE EDITORS
AND AUTHORS

Dr. Carla C. Johnson is a Professor of Science Education and Office of Research and Innovation Faculty Research Fellow at North Carolina State University. Dr. Johnson has served (2015–2021) as the director of research and evaluation for the Department of Defense–funded Army Educational Outreach Program (AEOP), a global portfolio of STEM education programs, competitions, and apprenticeships. She has been a leader in STEM education for the past decade, serving as the director of STEM Centers, editor of the School Science and Mathematics journal, and lead researcher for the evaluation of Tennessee's Race to the Top–funded STEM portfolio. Dr. Johnson has published over 200 articles, books, book chapters, and curriculum books focused on STEM education. She is a former science and social studies teacher and was the recipient of the 2013 Outstanding Science Teacher Educator of the Year award from the Association for Science Teacher Education (ASTE), the 2012 Award for Excellence in Integrating Science and Mathematics from the School Science and Mathematics Association (SSMA), the 2014 award for best paper on Implications of Research for Educational Practice from ASTE, and the 2006 Outstanding Early Career Scholar Award from SSMA. Her research focuses on STEM education policy implementation, effective science teaching, and integrated STEM approaches.

Dr. Janet B. Walton is a senior research scholar at NC State University's College of Education in Raleigh, North Carolina. Dr. Walton served as assistant director of research and evaluation for the Army Educational Outreach Program (AEOP) from 2015 through 2021. She leverages backgrounds in economic development and education to develop K–12 curricular materials that integrate real-life issues with sound cross-curricular content and provide students and educators with innovative resources and curricular materials. Her research focuses include collaboration between schools and community stakeholders for STEM education, problem- and project-based learning pedagogies, online learning, and mixed methods research methodologies.

Dr. Erin E. Peters-Burton is the Donna R. and David E. Sterling endowed professor in science education at George Mason University in Fairfax, Virginia. She uses her experiences from 15 years as an engineer and secondary science, engineering, and mathematics teacher to develop research projects that directly inform classroom practice in science and engineering. Her research agenda is based on the idea that all students should build self-awareness of how they learn science and engineering. She works to help students see themselves as "science-minded" and help teachers create classrooms that support student skills to develop scientific knowledge. To accomplish this, she pursues research projects that investigate ways that students and teachers can use self-regulated learning theory in science and engineering, as well as how inclusive STEM schools can help students succeed. She received the Outstanding Science Teacher Educator of the Year award from ASTE in 2016 and a Teacher of Distinction Award and a Scholarly Achievement Award from George Mason University in 2012, and in 2010 she was named University Science Educator of the Year by the Virginia Association of Science Teachers.

Dr. Toni A. May is an associate professor of assessment, research, and statistics in the School of Education at Drexel University in Philadelphia, Pennsylvania. Dr. May's research concentrates on assessment and evaluation in education, with a focus on K–12 STEM.

Dr. Tamara J. Moore is an associate professor of engineering education in the College of Engineering at Purdue University. Dr. Moore's research focuses on defining STEM integration through the use of engineering as the connection and investigating its power for student learning.

Paula Schoeff taught grades K–8 for 20 years in Indiana and Ohio and assisted in helping educate teachers in Ohio and Kentucky in STEM practices. Schoeff has a master's degree from the University of Cincinnati in curriculum and instruction with a focus on science.

ACKNOWLEDGMENTS

This module was developed as a part of the STEM Road Map project (Carla C. Johnson, principal investigator). The Purdue University College of Education, General Motors, and other sources provided funding for this project.

See *www.routledge.com/9780367467524* for more information about *STEM Road Map: A Framework for Integrated STEM Education*.

PART 1

THE STEM ROAD MAP

BACKGROUND, THEORY, AND PRACTICE

OVERVIEW OF THE *STEM ROAD MAP CURRICULUM SERIES*

Carla C. Johnson, Erin Peters-Burton, and Tamara J. Moore

The *STEM Road Map Curriculum Series* was conceptualized and developed by a team of STEM educators from across the United States in response to a growing need to infuse real-world learning contexts, delivered through authentic problem-solving pedagogy, into K–12 classrooms. The curriculum series is grounded in integrated STEM, which focuses on the integration of the STEM disciplines – science, technology, engineering, and mathematics – delivered across content areas, incorporating the Framework for 21st Century Learning along with grade-level-appropriate academic standards. The curriculum series begins in kindergarten, with a five-week instructional sequence that introduces students to the STEM themes and gives them grade-level-appropriate topics and real-world challenges or problems to solve. The series uses project-based and problem-based learning, presenting students with the problem or challenge during the first lesson, and then teaching them science, social studies, English language arts, mathematics, and other content as they apply what they learn to the challenge or problem at hand.

Authentic assessment and differentiation are embedded throughout the modules. Each *STEM Road Map Curriculum Series* module has a lead discipline, which may be science, social studies, English language arts, or mathematics. All disciplines are integrated into each module, along with ties to engineering. Another key component is the use of STEM Research Notebooks to allow students to track their own learning progress. The modules are designed with a scaffolded approach, with increasingly complex concepts and skills introduced as students progress through grade levels.

The developers of this work view the curriculum as a resource that is intended to be used either as a whole or in part to meet the needs of districts, schools, and teachers who are implementing an integrated STEM approach. A variety of

Carla C. Johnson et al.

implementation formats are possible, from using one stand-alone module at a given grade level to using all five modules to provide 25 weeks of instruction. Also, within each grade band (K–2, 3–5, 6–8, 9–12), the modules can be sequenced in various ways to suit specific needs.

STANDARDS-BASED APPROACH

The *STEM Road Map Curriculum Series* is anchored in the *Next Generation Science Standards* (*NGSS*), the *Common Core State Standards for Mathematics* (*CCSS Mathematics*), the *Common Core State Standards for English Language Arts* (*CCSS ELA*), and the Framework for 21st Century Learning. Each module includes a detailed curriculum map that incorporates the associated standards from the particular area correlated to lesson plans. The STEM Road Map has very clear and strong connections to these academic standards, and each of the grade-level topics was derived from the mapping of the standards to ensure alignment among topics, challenges or problems, and the required academic standards for students. Therefore, the curriculum series takes a standards-based approach and is designed to provide authentic contexts for application of required knowledge and skills.

THEMES IN THE *STEM ROAD MAP CURRICULUM SERIES*

The K–12 STEM Road Map is organized around five real-world STEM themes that were generated through an examination of the big ideas and challenges for society included in STEM standards and those that are persistent dilemmas for current and future generations:

- Cause and Effect

- Innovation and Progress

- The Represented World

- Sustainable Systems

- Optimizing the Human Experience

These themes are designed as springboards for launching students into an exploration of real-world learning situated within big ideas. Most important, the five STEM Road Map themes serve as a framework for scaffolding STEM learning across the K–12 continuum.

The themes are distributed across the STEM disciplines so that they represent the big ideas in science (Cause and Effect; Sustainable Systems), technology (Innovation and Progress; Optimizing the Human Experience), engineering (Innovation and Progress;

Sustainable Systems; Optimizing the Human Experience), and mathematics (The Represented World), as well as concepts and challenges in social studies and 21st century skills that are also excellent contexts for learning in English language arts. The process of developing themes began with the clustering of the *NGSS* performance expectations and the National Academy of Engineering's grand challenges for engineering, which led to the development of the challenge in each module and connections of the module activities to the *CCSS Mathematics* and *CCSS ELA* standards. We performed these mapping processes with large teams of experts and found that these five themes provided breadth, depth, and coherence to frame a high-quality STEM learning experience from kindergarten through 12th grade.

Cause and Effect

The concept of cause and effect is a powerful and pervasive notion in the STEM fields. It is the foundation of understanding how and why things happen as they do. Humans spend considerable effort and resources trying to understand the causes and effects of natural and have designed phenomena to gain better control over events and the environment and to be prepared to react appropriately. Equipped with the knowledge of a specific cause-and-effect relationship, we can lead better lives or contribute to the community by altering the cause, leading to a different effect. For example, if a person recognizes that irresponsible energy consumption leads to global climate change, that person can act to remedy his or her contribution to the situation. Although cause and effect is a core idea in the STEM fields, it can actually be difficult to determine. Students should be capable of understanding not only when evidence points to cause and effect but also when evidence points to relationships but not direct causality. The major goal of education is to foster students to be empowered, analytic thinkers, capable of thinking through complex processes to make important decisions. Understanding causality, as well as when it cannot be determined, will help students become better consumers, global citizens, and community members.

Innovation and Progress

One of the most important factors in determining whether humans will have a positive future is innovation. Innovation is the driving force behind progress, which helps create possibilities that did not exist before. Innovation and progress are creative entities, but in the STEM fields, they are anchored by evidence and logic, and they use established concepts to move the STEM fields forward. In creating something new, students must consider what is already known in the STEM fields and apply this knowledge appropriately. When we innovate, we create value that was not there previously and we create new conditions and possibilities for even

more innovations. Students should consider how their innovations might affect progress and use their STEM thinking to change current human burdens to benefits. For example, if we develop more efficient cars that use byproducts from another manufacturing industry, such as food processing, then we have used waste productively and reduced the need for the waste to be hauled away, an indirect benefit of the innovation.

The Represented World

When we communicate about the world we live in, how the world works, and how we can meet the needs of humans, sometimes we can use the actual phenomena to explain a concept. Sometimes, however, the concept is too big, too slow, too small, too fast, or too complex for us to explain using the actual phenomena, and we must use a representation or a model to help communicate the important features. We need representations and models such as graphs, tables, mathematical expressions, and diagrams because it makes our thinking visible. For example, when examining geologic time, we cannot actually observe the passage of such large chunks of time, so we create a timeline or a model that uses a proportional scale to visually illustrate how much time has passed for different eras. Another example may be something too complex for students at a particular grade level, such as explaining the p subshell orbitals of electrons to fifth graders. Instead, we use the Bohr model, which more closely represents the orbiting of planets and is accessible to fifth graders.

When we create models, they are helpful because they point out the most important features of a phenomenon. We also create representations of the world with mathematical functions, which help us change parameters to suit the situation. Creating representations of a phenomenon engages students because they are able to identify the important features of that phenomenon and communicate them directly. But because models are estimates of a phenomenon, they leave out some of the details, so it is important for students to evaluate their usefulness as well as their shortcomings.

Sustainable Systems

From an engineering perspective, the term *system* refers to the use of "concepts of component need, component interaction, systems interaction, and feedback. The interaction of subcomponents to produce a functional system is a common lens used by all engineering disciplines for understanding, analysis, and design." (Koehler, Bloom, & Binns, 2013, p. 8). Systems can be either open (e.g., an ecosystem) or closed (e.g., a car battery). Ideally, a system should be sustainable, able to maintain equilibrium without much energy from outside the structure. Looking at a garden, we see flowers blooming, weeds sprouting, insects buzzing, and various forms of life living within its boundaries. This is an example of an ecosystem, a collection of living organisms that survive together, functioning as a system. The interaction of the organisms within the system and the influences of the environment (e.g., water, sunlight) can maintain the system for a period of time, thus demonstrating its ability to endure. Sustainability is a desirable feature of a system because it allows for existence of the entity in the long term.

In the STEM Road Map project, we identified different standards that we consider to be oriented toward systems that students should know and understand in the K–12 setting. These include ecosystems, the rock cycle, Earth processes (such as erosion, tectonics, ocean currents, weather phenomena), Earth-Sun-Moon cycles, heat transfer, and the interaction among the geosphere, biosphere, hydrosphere, and atmosphere. Students and teachers should understand that we live in a world of systems that are not independent of each other, but rather are intrinsically linked such that a disruption in one part of a system will have reverberating effects on other parts of the system.

Optimizing the Human Experience

Science, technology, engineering, and mathematics as disciplines have the capacity to continuously improve the ways humans live, interact, and find meaning in the world, thus working to optimize the human experience. This idea has two components: being more suited to our environment and being more fully human. For example, the progression of STEM ideas can help humans create solutions to complex problems, such as improving ways to access water sources, designing energy sources with minimal impact on our environment, developing new ways of communication and expression, and building efficient shelters. STEM ideas can also provide access to the secrets and wonders of nature. Learning in STEM requires students to think logically and systematically, which is a way of knowing the world that is markedly different from knowing the world as an artist. When students can employ various ways of knowing and understand when it is appropriate to use a different way of knowing or integrate ways of knowing, they are fully experiencing the best of what it is to be human. The problem-based learning scenarios provided in the STEM Road Map help students develop ways of thinking like STEM professionals as they ask questions and design solutions. They learn to optimize the human experience by innovating improvements in the designed world in which they live.

THE NEED FOR AN INTEGRATED STEM APPROACH

At a basic level, STEM stands for science, technology, engineering, and mathematics. Over the past decade, however, STEM has evolved to have a much broader scope and

implications. Now, educators and policy makers refer to STEM as not only a concentrated area for investing in the future of the United States and other nations but also as a domain and mechanism for educational reform.

The good intentions of the recent decade-plus of focus on accountability and increased testing has resulted in significant decreases not only in instructional time for teaching science and social studies but also in the flexibility of teachers to promote authentic, problem solving–focused classroom environments. The shift has had a detrimental impact on student acquisition of vitally important skills, which many refer to as 21st century skills, and often the ability of students to "think." Further, schooling has become increasingly siloed into compartments of mathematics, science, English language arts, and social studies, lacking any of the connections that are overwhelmingly present in the real world around children. Students have experienced school as content provided in boxes that must be memorized, devoid of any real-world context, and often have little understanding of why they are learning these things.

STEM-focused projects, curriculum, activities, and schools have emerged as a means to address these challenges. However, most of these efforts have continued to focus on the individual STEM disciplines (predominantly science and engineering) through more STEM classes and after-school programs in a "STEM enhanced" approach (Breiner et al., 2012). But in traditional and STEM enhanced approaches, there is little to no focus on other disciplines that are integral to the context of STEM in the real world. Integrated STEM education, on the other hand, infuses the learning of important STEM content and concepts with a much-needed emphasis on 21st century skills and a problem- and project-based pedagogy that more closely mirrors the real-world setting for society's challenges. It incorporates social studies, English language arts, and the arts as pivotal and necessary (Johnson, 2013; Rennie, Venville, & Wallace, 2012; Roehrig et al., 2012).

FRAMEWORK FOR STEM INTEGRATION IN THE CLASSROOM

The *STEM Road Map Curriculum Series* is grounded in the Framework for STEM Integration in the Classroom as conceptualized by Moore, Guzey, and Brown (2014) and Moore et al. (2014). The framework has six elements, described in the context of how they are used in the *STEM Road Map Curriculum Series* as follows:

1. The STEM Road Map contexts are meaningful to students and provide motivation to engage with the content. Together, these allow students to have different ways to enter into the challenge.

2. The STEM Road Map modules include engineering design that allows students to design technologies (i.e., products that are part of the designed world) for a compelling purpose.

3. The STEM Road Map modules provide students with the opportunities to learn from failure and redesign based on the lessons learned.

4. The STEM Road Map modules include standards-based disciplinary content as the learning objectives.

5. The STEM Road Map modules include student-centered pedagogies that allow students to grapple with the content, tie their ideas to the context, and learn to think for themselves as they deepen their conceptual knowledge.

6. The STEM Road Map modules emphasize 21st century skills and, in particular, highlight communication and teamwork.

All of the STEM Road Map modules incorporate these six elements; however, the level of emphasis on each of these elements varies based on the challenge or problem in each module.

THE NEED FOR THE *STEM ROAD MAP CURRICULUM SERIES*

As focus is increasing on integrated STEM, and additional schools and programs decide to move their curriculum and instruction in this direction, there is a need for high-quality, research-based curriculum designed with integrated STEM at the core. Several good resources are available to help teachers infuse engineering or more STEM enhanced approaches, but no curriculum exists that spans K–12 with an integrated STEM focus. The next chapter provides detailed information about the specific pedagogy, instructional strategies, and learning theory on which the *STEM Road Map Curriculum Series* is grounded.

REFERENCES

Breiner, J., Harkness, M., Johnson, C. C., & Koehler, C. (2012). What is STEM? A discussion about conceptions of STEM in education and partnerships. *School Science and Mathematics, 112*(1), 3–11.

Johnson, C. C. (2013). Conceptualizing integrated STEM education: Editorial. *School Science and Mathematics, 113*(8), 367–368.

Koehler, C. M., Bloom, M. A., & Binns, I. C. (2013). Lights, camera, action: Developing a methodology to document mainstream films' portrayal of nature of science and scientific inquiry. *Electronic Journal of Science Education, 17*(2).

Moore, T. J., Guzey, S. S., & Brown, A. (2014). Greenhouse design to increase habitable land: An engineering unit. *Science Scope*, 51–57.

Moore, T. J., Stohlmann, M. S., Wang, H.-H., Tank, K. M., Glancy, A. W., & Roehrig, G. H. (2014). Implementation and integration of engineering in K–12 STEM education. In S. Purzer, J. Strobel, & M. Cardella (Eds.), *Engineering in pre-college settings: Synthesizing research, policy, and practices* (pp. 35–60). West Lafayette, IN: Purdue Press.

Rennie, L., Venville, G., & Wallace, J. (2012). *Integrating science, technology, engineering, and mathematics: Issues, reflections, and ways forward*. New York: Routledge.

Roehrig, G. H., Moore, T. J., Wang, H. H., & Park, M. S. (2012). Is adding the *E* enough? Investigating the impact of K–12 engineering standards on the implementation of STEM integration. *School Science and Mathematics*, 112(1), 31–44.

STRATEGIES USED IN THE *STEM ROAD MAP CURRICULUM SERIES*

Erin Peters-Burton, Carla C. Johnson, Toni A. Sondergeld, and Tamara J. Moore

The *STEM Road Map Curriculum Series* uses what has been identified through research as best-practice pedagogy, including embedded formative assessment strategies throughout each module. This chapter briefly describes the key strategies that are employed in the series.

PROJECT- AND PROBLEM-BASED LEARNING

Each module in the *STEM Road Map Curriculum Series* uses either project-based learning or problem-based learning to drive the instruction. Project-based learning begins with a driving question to guide student teams in addressing a contextualized local or community problem or issue. The outcome of project-based instruction is a product that is conceptualized, designed, and tested through a series of scaffolded learning experiences (Blumenfeld et al., 1991; Krajcik & Blumenfeld, 2006). Problem-based learning is often grounded in a fictitious scenario, challenge, or problem (Barell, 2006; Lambros, 2004). On the first day of instruction within the unit, student teams are provided with the context of the problem. Teams work through a series of activities and use open-ended research to develop their potential solution to the problem or challenge, which need not be a tangible product (Johnson, 2003).

ENGINEERING DESIGN PROCESS

The *STEM Road Map Curriculum Series* uses engineering design as a way to facilitate integrated STEM within the modules. The engineering design process (EDP) is depicted in Figure 2.1 (p. 12). It highlights two major aspects of engineering design – problem scoping and solution generation – and six specific components of working toward a design: define the problem, learn about the problem, plan a solution, try the solution, test the solution, decide whether the solution is good enough. It also shows that communication and teamwork are involved throughout the entire process. As

Figure 2.1 Engineering Design Process

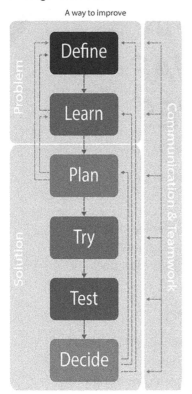

©2015 Picturestem, Purdue University Research Foundation

the arrows in the figure indicate, the order in which the components of engineering design are addressed depends on what becomes needed as designers progress through the EDP. Designers must communicate and work in teams throughout the process. The EDP is iterative, meaning that components of the process can be repeated as needed until the design is good enough to present to the client as a potential solution to the problem.

Problem scoping is the process of gathering and analyzing information to deeply understand the engineering design problem. It includes defining the problem and learning about the problem. Defining the problem includes identifying the problem, the client, and the end user of the design. The client is the person (or people) who hired the designers to do the work, and the end user is the person (or people) who will use the final design. The designers must also identify the criteria and the constraints of the problem. The criteria are the things the client wants from the solution, and the constraints are the things that limit the possible solutions. The designers must spend significant time learning about the problem, which can include activities such as the following:

- Reading informational texts and researching about relevant concepts or contexts

- Identifying and learning about needed mathematical and scientific skills, knowledge, and tools

- Learning about things done previously to solve similar problems

- Experimenting with possible materials that could be used in the design.

Problem scoping also allows designers to consider how to measure the success of the design in addressing specific criteria and staying within the constraints over multiple iterations of solution generation.

Solution generation includes planning a solution, trying the solution, testing the solution, and deciding whether the solution is good enough. Planning the solution includes generating many design ideas that both address the criteria and meet the constraints. Here the designers must consider what was learned about the problem during problem scoping. Design plans include clear communication of design ideas through media such as notebooks, blueprints, schematics, or storyboards. They also include details about the design, such as measurements, materials, colors, costs of materials, instructions for how things fit together, and sets of directions. Making the decision about which design idea to move forward involves considering the trade-offs of each design idea.

Once a clear design plan is in place, the designers must try the solution. Trying the solution includes developing a prototype (a testable model) based on the plan generated. The prototype might be something physical or a process to accomplish a goal. This component of design requires that the designers consider the risk involved in implementing the design. The prototype developed must be tested. Testing the solution includes conducting fair tests that verify whether the plan is a solution that is good enough to meet the client and end user needs and wants. Data need to be collected about the results of the tests of the prototype, and these data should be used to make evidence-based decisions regarding the design choices made in the plan. Here, the designers must again consider the criteria and constraints for the problem.

Using the data gathered from the testing, the designers must decide whether the solution is good enough to meet the client and end user needs and wants by assessment based on the criteria and constraints. Here, the designers must justify or reject design decisions based on the background research gathered while learning about the problem and on the evidence gathered during the testing of the solution. The designers must now decide whether to present the current solution to the client as a possibility or to do more iterations of design on the solution. If they decide that improvements need to be made to the solution, the designers must decide if there is more that needs to be understood about the problem, client, or end user; if another design idea should be tried; or if more planning needs to be conducted on the same design. One way or another, more work needs to be done.

Throughout the process of designing a solution to meet a client's needs and wants, designers work in teams and must communicate to each other, the client, and likely the end user. Teamwork is important in engineering design because multiple perspectives and differing skills and knowledge are valuable when working to solve problems. Communication is key to the success of the designed solution. Designers must communicate their ideas clearly using many different representations, such as text in an engineering notebook, diagrams, flowcharts, technical briefs, or memos to the client.

LEARNING CYCLE

The same format for the learning cycle is used in all grade levels throughout the STEM Road Map, so that students engage in a variety of activities to learn about phenomena in the modules thoroughly and have consistent experiences in the

problem- and project-based learning modules. Expectations for learning by younger students are not as high as for older students, but the format of the progression of learning is the same. Students who have learned with curriculum from the STEM Road Map in early grades know what to expect in later grades. The learning cycle consists of five parts – Introductory Activity/Engagement, Activity/Exploration, Explanation, Elaboration/Application of Knowledge, and Evaluation/Assessment – and is based on the empirically tested 5E model from BSCS (Bybee et al., 2006).

In the Introductory Activity/Engagement phase, teachers introduce the module challenge and use a unique approach designed to pique students' curiosity. This phase gets students to start thinking about what they already know about the topic and begin wondering about key ideas. The Introductory Activity/ Engagement phase positions students to be confident about what they are about to learn, because they have prior knowledge, and clues them into what they don't yet know.

In the Activity/Exploration phase, the teacher sets up activities in which students experience a deeper look at the topics that were introduced earlier. Students engage in the activities and generate new questions or consider possibilities using preliminary investigations. Students work independently, in small groups, and in whole-group settings to conduct investigations, resulting in common experiences about the topic and skills involved in the real-world activities. Teachers can assess students' development of concepts and skills based on the common experiences during this phase.

During the Explanation phase, teachers direct students' attention to concepts they need to understand and skills they need to possess to accomplish the challenge. Students participate in activities to demonstrate their knowledge and skills to this point, and teachers can pinpoint gaps in student knowledge during this phase.

In the Elaboration/Application of Knowledge phase, teachers present students with activities that engage in higher-order thinking to create depth and breadth of student knowledge, while connecting ideas across topics within and across STEM. Students apply what they have learned thus far in the module to a new context or elaborate on what they have learned about the topic to a deeper level of detail.

In the last phase, Evaluation/Assessment, teachers give students summative feedback on their knowledge and skills as demonstrated through the challenge. This is not the only point of assessment (as discussed in the section on Embedded Formative Assessments), but it is an assessment of the culmination of the knowledge and skills for the module. Students demonstrate their cognitive growth at this point and reflect on how far they have come since the beginning of the module. The challenges are designed to be multidimensional in the ways students must collaborate and communicate their new knowledge.

STEM RESEARCH NOTEBOOK

One of the main components of the *STEM Road Map Curriculum Series* is the STEM Research Notebook, a place for students to capture their ideas, questions, observations, reflections, evidence of progress, and other items associated with their daily work. At the beginning of each module, the teacher walks students through the setup of the STEM Research Notebook, which could be a three-ring binder, composition book, or spiral notebook. You may wish to have students create divided sections so that they can easily access work from various disciplines during the module. Electronic notebooks kept on student devices are also acceptable and encouraged. Students will develop their own table of contents and create chapters in the notebook for each module.

Each lesson in the *STEM Road Map Curriculum Series* includes one or more prompts that are designed for inclusion in the STEM Research Notebook and appear as questions or statements that the teacher assigns to students. These prompts require students to apply what they have learned across the lesson to solve the big problem or challenge for that module. Each lesson is designed to meaningfully refer students to the larger problem or challenge they have been assigned to solve with their teams. The STEM Research Notebook is designed to be a key formative assessment tool, as students' daily entries provide evidence of what they are learning. The notebook can be used as a mechanism for dialogue between the teacher and students, as well as for peer and self-evaluation.

The use of the STEM Research Notebook is designed to scaffold student notebooking skills across the grade bands in the *STEM Road Map Curriculum Series*. In the early grades, children learn how to organize their daily work in the notebook as a way to collect their products for future reference. In elementary school, students structure their notebooks to integrate background research along with their daily work and lesson prompts. In the upper grades (middle and high school), students expand their use of research and data gathering through team discussions to more closely mirror the work of STEM experts in the real world.

THE ROLE OF ASSESSMENT IN THE *STEM ROAD MAP CURRICULUM SERIES*

Starting in the middle years and continuing into secondary education, the word *assessment* typically brings grades to mind. These grades may take the form of a letter or a percentage, but they typically are used as a representation of a student's content mastery. If well thought out and implemented, however, classroom assessment can offer teachers, parents, and students valuable information about student learning and misconceptions that does not necessarily come in the form of a grade (Popham, 2013).

The *STEM Road Map Curriculum Series* provides a set of assessments for each module. Teachers are encouraged to use assessment information for more than just assigning grades to students. Instead, assessments of activities requiring students to actively engage in their learning, such as student journaling in STEM Research Notebooks, collaborative presentations, and constructing graphic organizers, should be used to move student learning forward. Whereas other curriculum with assessments may include objective-type (multiple-choice or matching) tests, quizzes, or worksheets, we have intentionally avoided these forms of assessments to better align assessment strategies with teacher instruction and student learning techniques. Since the focus of this book is on project- or problem-based STEM curriculum and instruction that focuses on higher-level thinking skills, appropriate and authentic performance assessments were developed to elicit the most reliable and valid indication of growth in student abilities (Brookhart & Nitko, 2008).

Comprehensive Assessment System

Assessment throughout all STEM Road Map curriculum modules acts as a comprehensive system in which formative and summative assessments work together to provide teachers with high-quality information on student learning. Formative assessment occurs when the teacher finds out formally or informally what a student knows about a smaller, defined concept or skill and provides timely feedback to the student about his or her level of proficiency. Summative assessments occur when students have performed all activities in the module and are given a cumulative performance evaluation in which they demonstrate their growth in learning.

A comprehensive assessment system can be thought of as akin to a sporting event. Formative assessments are the practices: It is important to accomplish them consistently, they provide feedback to help students improve their learning, and making mistakes can be worthwhile if students are given an opportunity to learn from them. Summative assessments are the competitions: Students need to be prepared to perform at the best of their ability. Without multiple opportunities to practice skills along the way through formative assessments, students will not have the best chance of demonstrating growth in abilities through summative assessments (Black & Wiliam, 1998).

Embedded Formative Assessments

Formative assessments in this module serve two main purposes: to provide feedback to students about their learning and to provide important information for the teacher to inform immediate instructional needs. Providing feedback to students is particularly important when conducting problem- or project-based learning because students take on much of the responsibility for learning, and teachers must facilitate student learning in an informed way. For example, if students are required to conduct research for the Activity/Exploration phase but are not familiar with what constitutes a reliable resource, they may develop misconceptions based on poor information. When a teacher monitors this learning through formative assessments and provides specific feedback related to the instructional goals, students are less likely to develop incomplete or incorrect conceptions in their independent investigations. By using formative assessment to detect problems in student learning and then acting on this information, teachers help move student learning forward through these teachable moments.

Formative assessments come in a variety of formats. They can be informal, such as asking students probing questions related to student knowledge or tasks or simply observing students engaged in an activity to gather information about student skills. Formative assessments can also be formal, such as a written quiz or a laboratory practical. Regardless of the type, three key steps must be completed when using formative assessments (Sondergeld, Bell, & Leusner, 2010). First, the assessment is delivered to students so that teachers can collect data. Next, teachers analyze the data (student responses) to determine student strengths and areas that need additional support. Finally, teachers use the results from information collected to modify lessons and create learning environments that reinforce weak points in student learning. If student learning information is not used to modify instruction, the assessment cannot be considered formative in nature. Formative assessments can be about content, science process skills, or even learning skills. When a formative assessment focuses on content, it assesses student knowledge about the disciplinary core ideas from the *Next Generation Science Standards* (*NGSS*) or content objectives from *Common Core State Standards for Mathematics* (*CCSS Mathematics*) or *Common Core State Standards for English Language Arts* (*CCSS ELA*). Content-focused formative assessments ask students questions about declarative knowledge regarding the concepts they have been learning. Process skills formative assessments examine the extent to which a student can perform science and engineering practices from the *NGSS* or process objectives from *CCSS Mathematics* or *CCSS ELA*, such as constructing an argument. Learning skills can also be assessed formatively by asking students to reflect on the ways they learn best during a module and identify ways they could have learned more.

Assessment Maps

Assessment maps or blueprints can be used to ensure alignment between classroom instruction and assessment. If what students are learning in the classroom is not the same as the content on which they are assessed, the resultant judgment made on student learning will be invalid (Brookhart & Nitko, 2008). Therefore, the issue of

instruction and assessment alignment is critical. The assessment map for this book (found in Chapter 3) indicates by lesson whether the assessment should be completed as a group or on an individual basis, identifies the assessment as formative or summative in nature, and aligns the assessment with its corresponding learning objectives.

Note that the module includes far more formative assessments than summative assessments. This is done intentionally to provide students with multiple opportunities to practice their learning of new skills before completing a summative assessment. Note also that formative assessments are used to collect information on only one or two learning objectives at a time so that potential relearning or instructional modifications can focus on smaller and more manageable chunks of information. Conversely, summative assessments in the module cover many more learning objectives, as they are traditionally used as final markers of student learning. This is not to say that information collected from summative assessments cannot or should not be used formatively. If teachers find that gaps in student learning persist after a summative assessment is completed, it is important to revisit these existing misconceptions or areas of weakness before moving on (Black et al., 2003).

SELF-REGULATED LEARNING THEORY IN THE STEM ROAD MAP MODULES

Many learning theories are compatible with the STEM Road Map modules, such as constructivism, situated cognition, and meaningful learning. However, we feel that the self-regulated learning theory (SRL) aligns most appropriately (Zimmerman, 2000). SRL requires students to understand that thinking needs to be motivated and managed (Ritchhart, Church, & Morrison, 2011). The STEM Road Map modules are student centered and are designed to provide students with choices, concrete hands-on experiences, and opportunities to see and make connections, especially across subjects (Eliason & Jenkins, 2012; NAEYC, 2016). Additionally, SRL is compatible with the modules because it fosters a learning environment that supports students' motivation, enables students to become aware of their own learning strategies, and requires reflection on learning while experiencing the module (Peters & Kitsantas, 2010).

The theory behind SRL (see Figure 2.2) explains the different processes that students engage in before, during, and after a learning task. Because SRL is a cyclical learning process, the accomplishment of one cycle develops strategies for the next learning cycle. This cyclic way of learning aligns with the various sections in the STEM Road Map lesson plans on Introductory Activity/ Engagement, Activity/ Exploration, Explanation, Elaboration/Application of Knowledge, and Evaluation/ Assessment. Since the students engaged in a module take on much of the

Figure 2.2 SRL Theory

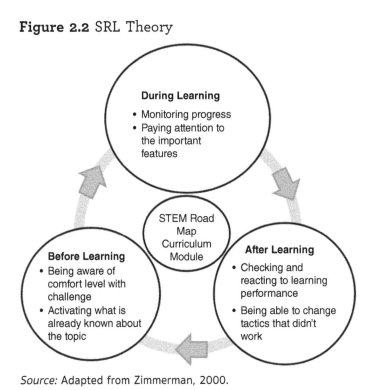

During Learning
- Monitoring progress
- Paying attention to the important features

STEM Road Map Curriculum Module

Before Learning
- Being aware of comfort level with challenge
- Activating what is already known about the topic

After Learning
- Checking and reacting to learning performance
- Being able to change tactics that didn't work

Source: Adapted from Zimmerman, 2000.

responsibility for learning, this theory also provides guidance for teachers to keep students on the right track.

The remainder of this section explains how SRL theory is embedded within the five sections of each module and points out ways to support students in becoming independent learners of STEM while productively functioning in collaborative teams.

Before Learning: Setting the Stage

Before attempting a learning task such as the STEM Road Map modules, teachers should develop an understanding of their students' level of comfort with the process of accomplishing the learning and determine what they already know about the topic. When students are comfortable with attempting a learning task, they tend to take more risks in learning and as a result achieve deeper learning (Bandura, 1986).

The STEM Road Map curriculum modules are designed to foster excitement from the very beginning. Each module has an Introductory Activity/Engagement section that introduces the overall topic from a unique and exciting perspective, engaging the students to learn more so that they can accomplish the challenge. The Introductory Activity also has a design component that helps teachers assess what students already know about the topic of the module. In addition to the deliberate designs in the lesson plans to support SRL, teachers can support a high level of student comfort with the learning challenge by finding out if students have ever accomplished the same kind of task and, if so, asking them to share what worked well for them.

During Learning: Staying the Course

Some students fear inquiry learning because they aren't sure what to do to be successful (Peters, 2010). However, the STEM Road Map curriculum modules are embedded with tools to help students pay attention to knowledge and skills that are important for the learning task and to check student understanding along the way.

One of the most important processes for learning is the ability for learners to monitor their own progress while performing a learning task (Peters, 2012). The modules allow students to monitor their progress with tools such as the STEM Research Notebooks, in which they record what they know and can check whether they have acquired a complete set of knowledge and skills. The STEM Road Map modules support inquiry strategies that include previewing, questioning, predicting, clarifying, observing, discussing, and journaling (Morrison & Milner, 2014). Through the use of technology throughout the modules, inquiry is supported by providing students access to resources and data while enabling them to process information, report the findings, collaborate, and develop 21st century skills.

It is important for teachers to encourage students to have an open mind about alternative solutions and procedures (Milner & Sondergeld, 2015) when working through the STEM Road Map curriculum modules. Novice learners can have difficulty knowing what to pay attention to and tend to treat each possible avenue for information as equal (Benner, 1984). Teachers are the mentors in a classroom and can point out ways for students to approach learning during the Activity/ Exploration, Explanation, and Elaboration/Application of Knowledge portions of the lesson plans to ensure that students pay attention to the important concepts and skills throughout the module. For example, if a student is to demonstrate conceptual awareness of motion when working on roller coaster research, but the student has misconceptions about motion, the teacher can step in and redirect student learning.

After Learning: Knowing What Works

The classroom is a busy place, and it may often seem that there is no time for self-reflection on learning. Although skipping this reflective process may save time in the short term, it reduces the ability to take into account things that worked well and things that didn't so that teaching the module may be improved next time. In the long run, SRL skills are critical for students to become independent learners who can adapt to new situations. By investing the time it takes to teach students SRL skills, teachers can save time later, because students will be able to apply methods and approaches for learning that they have found effective to new situations. In the Evaluation/Assessment portion of the STEM Road Map curriculum modules, as well as in the formative assessments throughout the modules, two processes in the after-learning phase are supported: evaluating one's own performance and accounting for ways to adapt tactics that didn't work well. Students have many opportunities to self-assess in formative assessments, both in groups and individually, using the rubrics provided in the modules.

The designs of the *NGSS* and *CCSS* allow for students to learn in diverse ways, and the STEM Road Map curriculum modules emphasize that students can use a variety of tactics to complete the learning process. For example, students can use STEM

Research Notebooks to record what they have learned during the various research activities. Notebook entries might include putting objectives in students' own words, compiling their prior learning on the topic, documenting new learning, providing proof of what they learned, and reflecting on what they felt successful doing and what they felt they still needed to work on. Perhaps students didn't realize that they were supposed to connect what they already knew with what they learned. They could record this and would be prepared in the next learning task to begin connecting prior learning with new learning.

SAFETY IN STEM

Student safety is a primary consideration in all subjects but is an area of particular concern in science, where students may interact with unfamiliar tools and materials that may pose additional safety risks. It is important to implement safety practices within the context of STEM investigations, whether in a classroom laboratory or in the field. When you keep safety in mind as a teacher, you avoid many potential issues with the lesson while also protecting your students.

STEM safety practices encompass things considered in the typical science class-room. Ensure that students are familiar with basic safety considerations, such as wearing protective equipment (e.g., safety glasses or goggles and latex-free gloves) and taking care with sharp objects, and know emergency exit procedures. Teachers should learn beforehand the locations of the safety eyewash, fume hood, fire extinguishers, and emergency shut-off switch in the classroom and how to use them. Also be aware of any school or district safety policies that are in place and apply those that align with the work being conducted in the lesson. It is important to review all safety procedures annually.

STEM investigations should always be supervised. Each lesson in the modules includes teacher guidelines for applicable safety procedures that should be followed. Before each investigation, teachers should go over these safety procedures with the student teams. Some STEM focus areas such as engineering require that students can demonstrate how to properly use equipment in the maker space before the teacher allows them to proceed with the lesson.

Information about classroom science safety, including a safety checklist for science classrooms, general lab safety recommendations, and links to other science safety resources, is available at the Council of State Science Supervisors (CSSS) website at *www.csss-science.org/safety.shtml*. The National Science Teachers Association (NSTA) provides a list of science rules and regulations, including standard operating procedures for lab safety, and a safety acknowledgement form for students and parents or guardians to sign. You can access these resources at *http://static.nsta.org/ pdfs/SafetyInTheScienceClassroom.pdf*. In addition, NSTA's Safety in the Science

Classroom web page (*www.nsta.org/safety*) has numerous links to safety resources, including papers written by the NSTA Safety Advisory Board.

Disclaimer: The safety precautions for each activity are based on use of the recommended materials and instructions, legal safety standards, and better professional practices. Using alternative materials or procedures for these activities may jeopardize the level of safety and therefore is at the user's own risk.

REFERENCES

Bandura, A. (1986). *Social foundations of thought and action: A social cognitive theory.* Englewood Cliffs, NJ: Prentice-Hall.

Barell, J. (2006). *Problem-based learning: An inquiry approach.* Thousand Oaks, CA: Corwin Press.

Benner, P. (1984). *From novice to expert: Excellence and power in clinical nursing practice.* Menlo Park, CA: Addison-Wesley Publishing Company.

Black, P., Harrison, C., Lee, C., Marshall, B., & Wiliam, D. (2003). *Assessment for learning: Putting it into practice.* Berkshire, UK: Open University Press.

Black, P., & Wiliam, D. (1998). Inside the black box: Raising standards through classroom assessment. *Phi Delta Kappan, 80*(2), 139–148.

Blumenfeld, P., Soloway, E., Marx, R., Krajcik, J., Guzdial, M., & Palincsar, A. (1991). Motivating project-based learning: Sustaining the doing, supporting learning. *Educational Psychologist, 26*(3), 369–398.

Brookhart, S. M., & Nitko, A. J. (2008). *Assessment and grading in classrooms.* Upper Saddle River, NJ: Pearson.

Bybee, R., Taylor, J., Gardner, A., Van Scotter, P., Carlson, J., Westbrook, A., & Landes, N. (2006). *The BSCS 5E instructional model: Origins and effectiveness. http://science.education.nih.gov/houseofreps.nsf/ b82d55fa138783c2852572c9004f5566/$FILE/Appendix?D.pdf.*

Eliason, C. F., & Jenkins, L. T. (2012). *A practical guide to early childhood curriculum.* 9th ed. New York: Merrill.

Johnson, C. (2003). Bioterrorism is real-world science: Inquiry-based simulation mirrors real life. *Science Scope, 27*(3), 19–23.

Krajcik, J., & Blumenfeld, P. (2006). Project-based learning. In R. Keith Sawyer (ed.), *The Cambridge handbook of the learning sciences* (pp. 317–334). New York: Cambridge University Press.

Lambros, A. (2004). *Problem-based learning in middle and high school classrooms: A teacher's guide to implementation.* Thousand Oaks, CA: Corwin Press.

Milner, A. R., & Sondergeld, T. (2015). Gifted urban middle school students: The inquiry continuum and the nature of science. *National Journal of Urban Education and Practice, 8*(3), 442–461.

Morrison, V., & Milner, A. R. (2014). Literacy in support of science: A closer look at cross-curricular instructional practice. *Michigan Reading Journal, 46*(2), 42–56.

National Association for the Education of Young Children. (NAEYC). (2016). Developmentally appropriate practice position statements. *www.naeyc.org/positionstatements/dap*.

Peters, E. E. (2010). Shifting to a student-centered science classroom: An exploration of teacher and student changes in perceptions and practices. *Journal of Science Teacher Education, 21*(3), 329–349.

Peters, E. E. (2012). Developing content knowledge in students through explicit teaching of the nature of science: Influences of goal setting and self-monitoring. *Science and Education, 21*(6), 881–898.

Peters, E. E., & Kitsantas, A. (2010). The effect of nature of science metacognitive prompts on science students' content and nature of science knowledge, metacognition, and self-regulatory efficacy. *School Science and Mathematics, 110*, 382–396.

Popham, W. J. (2013). *Classroom assessment: What teachers need to know.* 7th ed. Upper Saddle River, NJ: Pearson.

Ritchhart, R., Church, M. & Morrison, K. (2011). *Making thinking visible: How to promote engagement, understanding, and independence for all learners.* San Francisco, CA: Jossey-Bass.

Sondergeld, T. A., Bell, C. A., & Leusner, D. M. (2010). Understanding how teachers engage in formative assessment. *Teaching and Learning, 24*(2), 72–86.

Zimmerman, B. J. (2000). Attaining self-regulation: A social-cognitive perspective. In M. Boekaerts, P. Pintrich, & M. Zeidner (eds.), *Handbook of self-regulation* (pp. 13–39). San Diego: Academic Press.

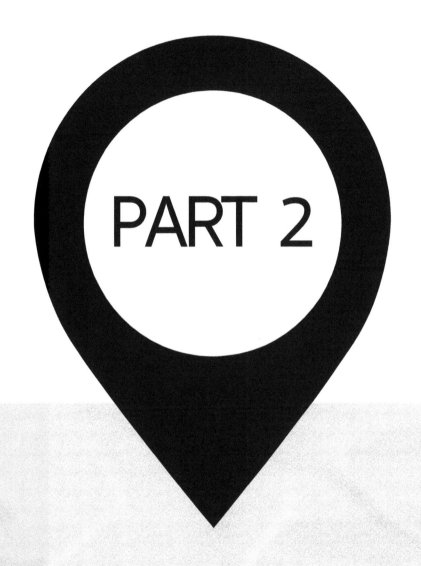

HYDROPOWER EFFICIENCY

STEM ROAD MAP MODULE

HYDROPOWER EFFICIENCY MODULE OVERVIEW

Paula Schoeff, Janet B. Walton, Carla C. Johnson, and Erin E. Peters-Burton

THEME: Sustainable Systems
LEAD DISCIPLINE: Science

MODULE SUMMARY

In this module, students will examine the STEM aspects involved in making informed decisions about creating a highly efficient dam that has minimal impact on the environment. Students will explore the use of natural resources to provide energy needs, specifically hydropower. They will explore the workings of watermills, wind turbines, and generators. In social studies, students will learn about the various types of alternative hydropower sources, including wave power and tidal power, and track the progress of electrification in the United States on a timeline. In English language arts, students will research the positive and negative consequences of hydropower and make an informed decision about utilizing natural resources and present their ideas using an infographic poster (adapted from Capobianco, et al., 2015).

ESTABLISHED GOALS AND OBJECTIVES

At the conclusion of this module, students will be able to do the following:

- Use the engineering design process (EDP) to create a design for a dam

- Compare and contrast renewable power sources

- Evaluate power sources for efficiency

- Design and implement an investigation around a testable question

- Use data analysis as evidence to answer a question under investigation

- Compare and contrast first-person and third-person accounts of the same event

- Identify positive and negative consequences of human modifications of the environment

- Make informed and reasoned decisions by accessing and using information effectively

- Participate in a debate, using evidence-based arguments to support an opinion

CHALLENGE OR PROBLEM FOR STUDENTS TO SOLVE: BIG CHANGES FOR MILLSIDE CORNERS DESIGN CHALLENGE

Students are presented the challenge of converting an existing water-powered gristmill into a power source to convert the water in a river into electricity. They will investigate a number of mechanisms for converting potential energy into kinetic energy, then build a model for the projected dam project.

CONTENT STANDARDS ADDRESSED IN THIS STEM ROAD MAP MODULE

A full listing with descriptions of the standards this module addresses can be found in the appendix. Listings of the particular standards addressed within lessons are provided in a table for each lesson in Chapter 4.

STEM RESEARCH NOTEBOOK

Each student should maintain a STEM Research Notebook, which will serve as a place for students to organize their work throughout this module (see p. XX for more general discussion on setup and use of the notebook). All written work in the module should be included in the notebook, including records of students' thoughts and ideas, fictional accounts based on the concepts in the module, and records of student progress through the EDP. The notebooks may be maintained across subject areas, giving students the opportunity to see that although their classes may be separated during the school day, the knowledge they gain is connected. You may also wish to have students include the STEM Research Notebook Guidelines student handout on page XX in their notebooks.

Emphasize to students the importance of organizing all information in a Research Notebook. Explain to them that scientists and other researchers maintain detailed Research Notebooks in their work. These notebooks, which are crucial to researchers' work because they contain critical information and track the researchers' progress, are often considered legal documents for scientists who are pursuing patents or wish to provide proof of their discovery process.

STEM Research Notebook Guidelines

STEM professionals record their ideas, inventions, experiments, questions, observations, and other work details in notebooks so that they can use these notebooks to help them think about their projects and the problems they are trying to solve. You will each keep a STEM Research Notebook during this module that is like the notebooks that STEM professionals use. In this notebook, you will include all your work and notes about ideas you have. The notebook will help you connect your daily work with the big problem or challenge you are working to solve.

It is important that you organize your notebook entries under the following headings:

1. **Chapter Topic or Title of Problem or Challenge:** You will start a new chapter in your STEM Research Notebook for each new module. This heading is the topic or title of the big problem or challenge that your team is working to solve in this module.

2. **Date and Topic of Lesson Activity for the Day:** Each day, you will begin your daily entry by writing the date and the day's lesson topic at the top of a new page. Write the page number both on the page and in the table of contents.

3. **Information Gathered from Research:** This is information you find from outside resources such as websites or books.

4. **Information Gained from Class or Discussions with Team Members:** This information includes any notes you take in class and notes about things your team discusses. You can include drawings of your ideas here, too.

5. **New Data Collected from Investigations:** This includes data gathered from experiments, investigations, and activities in class.

6. **Documents:** These are handouts and other resources you may receive in class that will help you solve your big problem or challenge. Paste or staple these documents in your STEM Research Notebook for safekeeping and easy access later.

7. **Personal Reflections:** Here, you record your own thoughts and ideas on what you are learning.

8. **Lesson Prompts:** These are questions or statements that your teacher assigns you within each lesson to help you solve your big problem or challenge. You will respond to the prompts in your notebook.

9. **Other Items:** This section includes any other items your teacher gives you or other ideas or questions you may have.

MODULE LAUNCH

Introduce the module challenge by reading the story Big Changes for Millside Corners (see p. XX), which explains the need to convert the community mill on Empire Creek into a hydroelectric power plant. Introduce students to the purpose of the product they will create (blog, podcast, or video) during the module and give students a list of engineers, inventors, environmentalists, humanitarians, and politicians. Have each student choose one person from the list and tell them that they will adopt this persona throughout the module in order to give the class opportunities to consider the problem of Millside Corners from a variety of perspectives.

PREREQUISITE SKILLS FOR THE MODULE

Students enter this module with a wide range of preexisting skills, information, and knowledge. Table 3.1 provides an overview of prerequisite skills and knowledge that students are expected to apply in this module, along with examples of how they apply this knowledge throughout the module. Differentiation strategies are also provided for students who may need additional support in acquiring or applying this knowledge.

Table 3.1 Prerequisite Key Knowledge and Examples of Applications and Examples of Application and Differentiation Strategies

Prerequisite Key Knowledge	Application of Knowledge	Differentiation for Students Needing Knowledge
Science		
• A force is a push or pull. • Gravity is a force that pulls objects toward the earth. • Ask questions, make logical predictions, plan investigations, and represent data. • Use senses and tools to make observations. • Communicate understanding of data using age-appropriate vocabulary.	• Students will identify and describe forces in a waterwheel. • Students will identify the forces interacting in a wind turbine, water wheel, and dam. • Students will select and use appropriate tools and equipment to conduct investigations. • Students will maintain a notebook that includes observations, data, diagrams, and reflections.	• Provide demonstrations and physical models of forces. • Provide opportunities to work in teams as students create and build models and tests. • Provide opportunities to use language orally and written to describe scientific processes and principles. • Select models and use appropriate tools and simple equipment to conduct an investigation.

Table 3.1 (*continued*)

Prerequisite Key Knowledge	Application of Knowledge	Differentiation for Students Needing Knowledge
	• Students will analyze and communicate findings from multiple investigations of similar phenomena to reach a conclusion.	• Provide samples of STEM research notebook pages. • Scaffold student efforts to organize data into appropriate tables, graphs, drawings, or diagrams by providing step-by-step instructions. • Identify specific investigations that could be used to answer a particular question and identify reasons for this choice.
Mathematics		
• Add, subtract, multiply, and divide two-digit whole numbers accurately. • Convert fractions into decimals • Measure volume and distance with appropriate tools and units. • Make precise measurements.	• Students will use math operations when creating tables and graphs. • Students will make measurements on a ruler and convert it into its decimal equivalent. • Students will convert data between different units of measure. • Students will measure volumes of water using cylinders and measuring cups. • Students will indicate the units of measure as they measure objects.	• Review properties of operations using examples of volume and distance. • Utilize textbook support, teacher instruction, models, graphic organizers, and online instruction to provide practice. • Provide opportunities to practice measuring with precision, using the correct units. • Provide a table which offers a visual reinforcement for measurements and units. • Provide instruction in use of cylinders and measuring cups for finding volume.
English Language Arts		
Reading • Use information gained from illustrations and text to build understanding of scientific content.	*Reading* • Students will research and report how water has been used to produce energy.	*Reading* • Provide reading strategies to support comprehension of non-fiction texts, including using vocabulary notecards, creating graphic

Table 3.1 (*continued*)

Prerequisite Key Knowledge	Application of Knowledge	Differentiation for Students Needing Knowledge
• Use information gained from illustrations and text to build understanding of how dams work.	• Students will use the Internet and textbooks to map the historical development of renewable energy sources on a timeline.	organizers, writing about research in a STEM research notebook, and discussing topics.
Writing • Use science terms to inform and explain thoughts and ideas about the topic. • Use key terminology as words and pictures. • Provide evidence to support ideas and opinions about topics.	*Writing* • Write informative and explanatory narratives to convey ideas and information clearly. • Write narratives to describe experiences using effective techniques, descriptive details, and clear event sequences.	*Writing* • Provide a template for writing. • Provide writing organization worksheets to scaffold student work. • Provide rubrics that have a consistent format so students can measure their own writing.
Communication • Participate in collaborative conversations using appropriate language and skills. • Effectively support scientific knowledge with appropriate language and relevant, descriptive details.	*Communication* • Students will engage in a number of collaborative discussions in which they will convey and support learning. • Students will write in a blog platform to respond to scientific topics. • Students will create an infographic to indicate informed use of natural resources to generate power.	*Communication* • Scaffold student understanding of communication skills by providing examples of appropriate language and presentation. • Provide worksheets and rubrics to support organization of facts and use of relevant descriptive details.

POTENTIAL STEM MISCONCEPTIONS

Students enter the classroom with a wide variety of prior knowledge and ideas, so it is important to be alert to misconceptions, or inappropriate understandings of foundational knowledge. These misconceptions can be classified as one of several types: "preconceived notions," opinions based on popular beliefs or understandings; "nonscientific beliefs," knowledge students have gained about science from sources outside the scientific community; "conceptual misunderstandings," incorrect conceptual models based on incomplete understanding of concepts; "vernacular misconceptions," misunderstandings of words based on their common use versus their scientific use; and "factual misconceptions," incorrect or imprecise knowledge learned in early life that remains unchallenged (NRC, 1997, p. 28). Misconceptions must be addressed and dismantled for students to reconstruct their knowledge, and therefore teachers should be prepared to take the following steps:

- Identify students' misconceptions.

- Provide a forum for students to confront their misconceptions.

- Help students reconstruct and internalize their knowledge, based on scientific models (NRC, 1997, p. 29).

Keeley and Harrington (2010) recommend using diagnostic tools such as probes and formative assessment to identify and confront student misconceptions and begin the process of reconstructing student knowledge. Keeley's (2005) *Uncovering Student Ideas in Science* series contains probes targeted toward uncovering student misconceptions in a variety of areas and may be useful resources for addressing student misconceptions in this module. Some commonly held misconceptions specific to lesson content are provided with each lesson so that you can be alert for student misunderstanding of the science concepts presented and used during this module.

SELF-REGULATED LEARNING (SRL) PROCESS COMPONENTS

Table 3.2 illustrates some of the activities in the Rainwater Analysis module and how they align to the SRL processes before, during, and after learning.

Table 3.2 SRL Learning Process Components

Learning Process Components	Example from Hydropower Module	Lesson Number and Learning Component
Before Learning		
Motivates students	Students take on the persona of a historical figure and consider the implications of building a hydropower system through this character.	Begins in Lesson 1 (Activity/Exploration) and throughout module

Table 3.2 (*continued*)

Learning Process Components	Example from Hydropower Module	Lesson Number and Learning Component
Evokes prior learning	Students read the story, *Energy Island*, and create a working definition of efficiency based on their background knowledge and concepts illustrated in the story.	Lesson 2 Introductory Activity/ Engagement
During Learning		
Focuses on important features	Students share their water wheel design with peers and make one change based on feedback.	Lesson 2 Elaboration/Application of Knowledge
Helps students monitor their progress	Students use their understanding of renewable energy resources to create an Infographic.	Lesson 3 Elaboration/Application of Knowledge
After Learning		
Evaluates learning	Students receive feedback on the written and sketch portion of their proposal in two different rubrics.	Lesson 4 Evaluation/Assessment
Takes account of what worked and what did not work	Students reflect on their learning in the module and create arguments and counterarguments either for or against a hydropower system.	Lesson 4 Explanation

INTEGRATING INSTRUCTION ACROSS SUBJECTS

The modules of the STEM Road Map take into account that logistics of instruction, such as scheduling and departmentalization, can make teaching integrated subject matter difficult. It is not uncommon, for example, for the same grade-level science and English language arts teachers to have completely different students, which makes integrating science content with content from other subjects difficult. However, we recognize that some schools allow for teachers from different content areas to team teach. The modules of the STEM Road Map Series are written to accommodate both situations – the singular teacher and the teachers who are able to team teach or integrate instruction across subjects in other ways. A teacher who is teaching the module by themselves may choose to follow only the lead subject, offering enrichment activities in the other connecting subjects. Teachers who are teaching the modules in a single subject course may also want to collaborate with their peers in the other disciplinary areas to get ideas for ways to incorporate the supporting connections seamlessly. Teachers who are able to teach an integrated curriculum can use the module as written for each of the four subjects in the Learning Plan Components sections of the module.

STRATEGIES FOR DIFFERENTIATING INSTRUCTION WITHIN THIS MODULE

For the purposes of this curriculum module, differentiated instruction is conceptualized as a way to tailor instruction – including process, content, and product – to various student needs in your class. A number of differentiation strategies are integrated into lessons across the module. The problem- and project-based learning approach used in the lessons are designed to address students' multiple intelligences by providing a variety of entry points and methods to investigate the key concepts in the module (for example, investigating rainwater and horticulture using scientific inquiry, fiction and nonfiction literature, journaling, and collaborative design). Differentiation strategies for students needing support in prerequisite knowledge can be found in Table 3.1 (p. XX). You are encouraged to use information gained about student prior knowledge during introductory activities and discussions to inform your instructional differentiation. Strategies incorporated into this lesson include flexible grouping, varied environmental learning contexts, assessments, compacting, tiered assignments and scaffolding, and mentoring.

Flexible Grouping: Students work collaboratively in a variety of activities throughout this module. Grouping strategies you may choose to employ include student-led grouping, placing students in groups according to ability level, grouping students randomly, grouping them so that students in each group have complementary strengths (for instance, one student might be strong in mathematics, another in art, and another in writing), or grouping students according to common interests.

Varied Environmental Learning Contexts: Students have the opportunity to learn in various contexts throughout the module, including alone, in groups, in quiet reading and research-oriented activities, and in active learning in inquiry and design activities. In addition, students learn in a variety of ways through doing inquiry activities, journaling, reading a variety of texts, watching videos, class discussion, and conducting web-based research.

Assessments: Students are assessed in a variety of ways throughout the module, including individual and collaborative formative and summative assessments. Students have the opportunity to produce work via written text, oral and media presentations, and modeling. You may choose to provide students with additional choices of media for their products (for example, PowerPoint presentations, posters, or student-created websites or blogs).

Compacting: Based on student prior knowledge, you may wish to adjust instructional activities for students who exhibit prior mastery of a learning objective. Because student work in science is largely collaborative throughout the module, this strategy may be most appropriate for mathematics, ELA, or social studies activities. You may wish to compile a classroom database of research resources and supplementary readings for a variety of reading levels and on a variety of topics related to the module's topic to provide opportunities for students to undertake independent reading.

Tiered Assignments and Scaffolding: Based on your awareness of student ability, understanding of concepts, and mastery of skills, you may wish to provide students with variations on activities by adding complexity to assignments or providing more or fewer learning supports for activities throughout the module. For instance, some students may need additional support in identifying key search words and phrases for web-based research or may benefit from cloze sentence handouts to enhance vocabulary understanding. Other students may benefit from expanded reading selections and additional reflective writing or from working with manipulatives and other visual representations of mathematical concepts. You may also work with your school librarian to compile a set of topical resources at a variety of reading levels.

Mentoring: As group design teamwork becomes increasingly complex throughout the module, you may wish to have a resource teacher, older student, or parent volunteer work with groups that struggle to stay on task and collaborate effectively.

STRATEGIES FOR ENGLISH LANGUAGE LEARNERS

Students who are developing proficiency in English language skills require additional supports to simultaneously learn academic content and the specialized language associated with specific content areas. WIDA (World-Class Instructional Design and Assessment) has created a framework for providing support to these students and makes available rubrics and guidance on differentiating instructional materials for

English language learners (ELLs) (see www.wida.us). In particular, ELL students may benefit from additional sensory supports such as images, physical modeling, and graphic representations of module content, as well as interactive support through collaborative work. This module incorporates a variety of sensory supports and offers ongoing opportunities for ELL students to work with collaboratively. The focus on dams affords an opportunity for ELL students to share culturally diverse experiences with geography and energy production.

Teachers differentiating instruction for ELL students should carefully consider the needs of these students as they introduce and use academic language in various language domains (listening, speaking, reading, and writing) throughout this module. To adequately differentiate instruction for ELL students, teachers should have an understanding of the proficiency level of each student. The following five overarching PreK–5 WIDA learning standards are relevant to this module:

- Standard 1: Social and Instructional Language. Focus on following directions, personal information, and collaboration with peers.

- Standard 2: The Language of Language Arts. Focus on nonfiction, fiction, sequence of story, and elements of story.

- Standard 3: The Language of Mathematics. Focus on basic operations, number sense, interpretation of data, and patterns.

- Standard 4: The Language of Science. Focus on forces in nature, scientific process, Earth and sky, living and nonliving things, organisms and environment, and weather.

SAFETY CONSIDERATIONS FOR THE ACTIVITIES IN THIS MODULE

This module's science component focuses on hydropower and the role of kinetic and potential energy in dam design. Ensure that water spilled on the floor is cleaned up promptly to avoid slipping. All laboratory occupants must wear safety glasses or goggles during all phases of inquiry activities (setup, hands-on investigation, and takedown). For more general safety guidelines, see the section on Safety in STEM in Chapter 2 (p. XX) and for lesson-specific safety information, see the Safety Notes section of each lesson in Chapter 4.

DESIRED OUTCOMES AND MONITORING SUCCESS

The desired outcomes for this module are outlined in Table 3.3, along with suggested ways to gather evidence to monitor student success. For more specific details on desired outcomes, see the Established Goals and Objectives sections for the module and individual lessons.

Table 3.3 Desired Outcomes and Evidence of Success in Achieving Identified Outcomes

Desired Outcome	Evidence of Success in Achieving Identified Outcome	
	Performance Tasks	Other Measures
• Students will be able to apply an understanding of how hydropower systems work to create a model of a dam and/or power plant and redesign elements of the model to improve efficiency.	• Students will maintain STEM research notebooks that will contain data from investigations, sketches, research notes, evidence of collaboration, and mathematics, ELA, and social studies related work. • Students will design a model of a hydropower system. • Students will be able to defend their design decisions. • Students will be assessed using project rubrics that focus on learning and application of skills related to the academic content.	• STEM research notebooks will be assessed using a STEM research notebook rubric. • Student collaboration will be evaluated using a self-assessment reflection form and peer feedback.

ASSESSMENT PLAN OVERVIEW AND MAP

Table 3.4 provides an overview of the major group and individual *products* and *deliverables*, or things that comprise the assessment for this module. Table 3.5 has a full assessment map of formative and summative assessments in this module.

Table 3.4 Major Products/Deliverables for Groups and Individuals

Lesson	Major Group Products/ Deliverables	Major Individual Products/ Deliverables
1	• Pinwheel activity • Wind Turbine Design Challenge • Electrification of the U.S. Research and Timeline	• Pinwheel activity observations • Wind Turbine Design Challenge data • Biographical essay of a historical figure
2	• Efficiency Activity • Water Wheel Design Challenge • Energy Research slideshow • Renewable Energy	• Efficiency Activity data • Water Wheel Design Challenge EDP booklet • Renewable Energy Research and Map • Blog posts
3	• Water Pressure Activity • Dam Design Challenge • OREO opinion essay • Infographics energy poster	• Water pressure data • Dam Design Challenge EDP booklet • OREO opinion essay • Blog posts

Table 3.4 (*continued*)

Lesson	Major Group Products/ Deliverables	Major Individual Products/ Deliverables
4	• Big Changes for Millside Corners models • Debate	• EDP booklet for Big Changes for Millside Corners models • Written Proposals for Big Changes for Millside Corners • Building an Argument handout

Table 3.5 Assessment Map for Hydropower Efficiency Module

Lesson	Assessment	Group/ Individual	Formative/ Summative	Lesson Objective Assessed (students will:)
1	Name that Force *game*	Group	Formative	• Identify work as what occurs when a force is applied over a distance • Identify potential and kinetic energy interactions of objects • Evaluate the energy source of activities
1	Pinwheel Activity *rubric*	Individual	Formative	• Identify potential and kinetic energy interactions of objects • Evaluate the energy source of activities
1	Wind Turbine Design Challenge *rubric*	Individual	Formative	• Utilize the design process (EDP) to design a model of a wind turbine
1	Electrification of the U.S. research and *timeline*	Group	Formative	• Trace the history of the electrification of the U.S. on a timeline.
1	Electrification of the U.S. presentation *rubric*	Group	Formative	• Describe several electrical inventions in the U.S. within their historical context
1	Biographical essay	Individual	Formative	• Understand the point of view of a historical figure
2	Energy Sorting Activity *Performance task*	Group	Formative	• Distinguish between renewable and nonrenewable energy sources and name several examples of each
2	Efficiency Activity *handout, rubric*	Individual	Formative	• Identify efficiency as the ratio of output energy to input energy • Compare and contrast the efficiency of devices

Table 3.5 (*continued*)

Lesson	Assessment	Group/ Individual	Formative/ Summative	Lesson Objective Assessed (students will:)
2	Renewable Energy *Research* and regional map *rubric*	Group	Formative	• Identify and describe how several sources of renewable energy are used across the U.S. • Use mapping skills to determine where natural resources are being accessed for energy usage.
2	Efficiency activity *performance activity* and *handout*	Group/ Individual	Formative	• Identify efficiency as the ratio of output energy to input energy • Compare and contrast the efficiency of devices • Explain how friction and heat are related to efficiency
2	Water Wheel Design Challenge *performance activity* and *handout*	Group/ Individual	Formative	• Identify the basic components of a water wheel • Utilize the design process (EDP) to build and improve the efficiency of a water wheel
2	Energy research *slideshow*	Group	Summative	• Identify and describe how several sources of renewable energy are used across the U.S. • Communicate their learning about renewable energy use in the U.S. to an audience using a slideshow
2	Blog posts, podcast or video script *rubric*	Individual	Formative	• Evaluate renewable energy resources from the perspective of an historical figure and communicate these ideas in writing
3	Water Pressure Activity *performance task* and *rubric*	Group/ Individual	Formative	• Describe the concept of water pressure and apply their understanding to predict the direction that water will flow in a pipe or field • Recognize that water pressure increases with water depth
3	Build a Dam Design Challenge	Group/ Individual	Formative	• Identify the parts of a dam • Apply the EDP to design a model of a dam

Table 3.5 (*continued*)

Lesson	Assessment	Group/ Individual	Formative/ Summative	Lesson Objective Assessed (students will:)
	performance activity and *rubric*			• Describe the concept of water pressure and apply their understanding to predict the direction that water will flow in a pipe or field
3	OREO opinion essay *rubric*	Individual	Summative	• Apply their understanding of energy sources to create an opinion essay
3	Infographics *rubric*	Group	Summative	• Apply their understanding of energy sources to create an infographic to explain the importance of utilizing renewable energy.
3	Blog posts, podcast or video script *rubric*	Individual	Formative	• Evaluate renewable energy resources from the perspective of an historical figure and communicate these ideas in writing
4	Big Changes for Millside Corner Design Challenge model *rubric*	Group	Summative	• Use the EDP to develop a model of a hydroelectric power plant and dam which maximizes the efficiency of water pressure • Effectively utilize shapes, materials, and measurements to create a model of a hydropower system
4	Big Changes for Millside Corner Design Challenge written proposal *rubric*	Individual	Summative	• Describe important details of a hydroelectric power plant and dam in a written proposal
4	Building an Argument *handout*	Individual	Summative	• Develop an argument to support an opinion using evidence
4	Hydropower Debate *rubric*	Group	Summative	• Participate in a debate using findings from their research

MODULE TIMELINE

Tables 3.6 to 3.10 (pp. 42–43) provide lesson timelines for each week of the module. The timelines are provided for general guidance only and are based on class times of approximately 45 minutes.

Table 3.6 STEM Road Map Module Schedule Week One

Day 1	Day 2	Day 3	Day 4	Day 5
Lesson 1 *Wind Wheels*	*Lesson 1* *Wind Wheels*	*Lesson 1* *Wind Wheels*	*Lesson 1* *Wind Wheels*	*Lesson 1* *Wind Wheels*
Introduce the module challenge. Class discussion about work; show *Name that Force* slideshow. Play the *Name that Force* game. Introduce historical figures' connection to module.	Pinwheel Activity.	Introduce EDP. Wind Turbine Challenge	Biographical Essay and Time Capsule activity.	Electrification of the U.S. activity.

Table 3.7 STEM Road Map Module Schedule Week Two

Day 6	Day 7	Day 8	Day 9	Day 10
Lesson 2 *Water Wheels*	*Lesson 2* *Water Wheels*	*Lesson 2* *Water Wheels*	*Lesson 2* *Water Wheels*	*Lesson 2* *Water Wheels*
Introduce natural resource use for energy. Read and discuss *Energy Island* by Allan Drummond.	Energy Sorting Activity. Introduce Efficiency Activity.	Efficiency Activity. Introduce Communicating in Millside Corners.	Renewable Energy Research and Mapping Activity.	Renewable Energy Research and Mapping Activity. Share Energy Research slideshows.

Table 3.8 STEM Road Map Module Schedule Week Three

Day 11	Day 12	Day 13	Day 14	Day 15
Lesson 2 *Water Wheels*	*Lesson 2* *Water Wheels*	*Lesson 3* *Under Pressure: Water Pressure and Dams*	*Lesson 3* *Under Pressure: Water Pressure and Dams*	*Lesson3* *Under Pressure: Water Pressure and Dams*
Share Energy Research slideshows. Water Wheel Design Challenge.	Student teams work to improve the efficiency of their water wheels. Renewable Energy Scavenger Hunt.	Students compare and contrast rivers and oceans and define altitude. Read (or watch video of) and discuss *Paddle to the Sea* by Holling C. Holling.	Continue discussion of *Paddle to the Sea*. Students explore water pressure simulation. Introduce Water Pressure Activity.	Water Pressure Activity. Introduce Build a Dam Design Challenge.

Table 3.9 STEM Road Map Module Schedule Week Four

Day 16	Day 17	Day 18	Day 19	Day 20
Lesson 3 Under Pressure: Water Pressure and Dams	*Lesson 3 Under Pressure: Water Pressure and Dams*	*Lesson 3 Under Pressure: Water Pressure and Dams*	*Lesson 4 The Big Changes for Millside Corners Design Challenge*	*Lesson 4 The Big Changes for Millside Corners Design Challenge*
Continue Build a Dam Design Challenge. Begin OREO Opinion Essay.	Continue Build a Dam Design Challenge. Continue OREO Opinion Essay. Introduce Energy Infographic Activity.	Continue OREO Opinion Essay. Continue Energy Infographic Activity.	Show and discuss the *Big Changes for Millside Corners* slideshow.	Student teams create models for the module challenge.

Table 3.10 STEM Road Map Module Schedule Week Five

Day 21	Day 22	Day 23	Day 24	Day 25
Lesson 4 The Big Changes for Millside Corners Design Challenge	*Lesson 4 The Big Changes for Millside Corners Design Challenge*	*Lesson 4 The Big Changes for Millside Corners Design Challenge*	*Lesson 4 The Big Changes for Millside Corners Design Challenge*	*Lesson 4 The Big Changes for Millside Corners Design Challenge*
Student teams continue working on models for the module challenge.	Student teams finish working on models for the module challenge. Students create written proposals for the module challenge.	Students complete their written proposals. Introduce and discuss debates. Students prepare for the debate by building their arguments.	Students finish preparing for the Millside Corners debate.	Hold Millside Corners debate.

Paula Schoeff et al.

RESOURCES

The media specialist can help teachers locate resources for students to view and read about hydropower, dams, and related content. Special educators and reading specialists can help find supplemental sources for students needing extra support in reading and writing. Additional resources may be found online. Community resources for this module may include city water plant workers or energy provider representatives, engineers, and environmental scientists.

REFERENCES

Capobianco, B. M., Parker, C., Laurier, A., & Rankin, J. (2015). The STEM road map for grades 3–5. In C. C. Johnson, E. E. Peters-Burton, & T. J. Moore (Eds.), *STEM Road Map: A framework for integrated STEM education* (pp. 68–95). New York: Routledge. *www.routledge.com/products/9781138804234*.

Keeley, P., & Harrington, R. (2010). *Uncovering student ideas in physical science; Volume 1: 45 new force and motion assessment probes.* Arlington, VA: NSTA Press.

National Research Council (NRC). (1997). *Science teaching reconsidered: A handbook.* Washington, DC: National Academies Press.

WIDA. (2020). *WIDA English language development standards framework, 2020 edition: Kindergarten–grade 12.* Board of Regents of the University of Wisconsin System. *https://wida.wisc.edu/sites/default/files/resource/WIDA-ELD-Standards-Framework-2020.pdf*

HYDROPOWER EFFICIENCY LESSON PLANS

Paula Schoeff, Janet B. Walton, Carla C. Johnson, and Erin E. Peters-Burton

Lesson Plan 1:
Wind Wheels

This lesson will introduce the students to the module and the module challenge, Big Changes for Millside Corners Design Challenge. Millside Corners is a fictional town that is facing a showdown between local factions over a proposed hydropower plant to be built in a local river. A force identification game will kick off the lesson to connect students to the physics definition of work and to introduce kinetic and potential energy. Student teams will be challenged to use the engineering design process (EDP) to build wind-powered devices that transfer energy from the force of moving air to mechanical rotation. Students will each research and discuss a historical figure whose perspective they will adopt as they consider issues surrounding the module challenge. Students will also trace the history of electrical energy in the U.S. and create a timeline that highlights important developments.

ESSENTIAL QUESTIONS

- What serves as proof that work has happened?

- What is the difference between force and energy?

- When does the phrase "energy cannot be created or destroyed" mean?

- What are the parts of a wind or water wheel?

- What is meant by *point of view*?

- Before electricity was widely available, what were the main forms of energy used in homes and businesses?

- How did the availability of electricity change life in communities?

ESTABLISHED GOALS AND OBJECTIVES

At the conclusion of this lesson, students will be able to do the following:

- Identify work as what occurs when a force is applied over a distance

- Identify potential and kinetic energy interactions of objects

- Evaluate the energy source of activities

- Utilize the engineering design process (EDP) to design a model of a wind turbine

- Trace the history of the electrification of the U.S. on a timeline

- Describe several electrical inventions in the U.S. within their historical context

- Understand the point of view of a historical figure

TIME REQUIRED

5 days (approximately 45 minutes each day; see Table 3.6).

MATERIALS

Required Materials for Lesson 1

- STEM Research Notebooks (for each student)

- Internet access

- Name that Force slideshow www.routledge.com/9781032618074

- Chart paper

- Markers

- Student handouts and teacher resources (attached at the end of lesson)

  - Teacher's Scoop on Millside Corners

  - Students' Scoop on Millside Corners

  - Pinwheel Activity student handout

  - EDP Applied to the Wind Turbine student handout

  - Wind Turbine Activity student handout

  - Historical Figures student handout

  - Biographical Essay/Time Capsule project

- Energy Sorting Activity

- Electrification of the United States Project Description

- Electrification of the United States Timeline student handout

- Electrical Inventions student handout

- Rubrics (attached at the end of lesson)

  - STEM Research Notebook Rubric

  - Collaboration Rubric

  - Pinwheel Activity Rubric

  - Wind Turbine Design Challenge Rubric

  - Biography Rubric

  - Electrification of the U.S. Presentation Rubric

Additional Materials for Working Forces Game

- Name that Force slideshow www.routledge.com/9781032618074

Additional Materials for Pinwheel Activity

- Toy pinwheel (for each pair of students)
- Small handheld fan (for class)

Additional Materials for Wind Turbine Challenge (for each team of 3–4 students)

- 1–3/16″ × 12″ dowel rod
- 10- ¼″ plastic straws
- 2 sheets of oak tag card stock or note cards
- empty plastic packaging such as milk jugs or soda bottles to be cut up as needed
- stapler
- scissors
- 12″ plastic ruler (w/ 3 holes)
- masking or duct tape
- glue sealer (such as Mod Podge)

- Additional materials depending on each team's design choices:
  - air dry modeling clay (also called, self-hardening clay)
  - plastic spoons
  - small craft straws or coffee stirrers
  - foil pie pan
  - craft sticks
  - large paper clips

Additional Materials for Time Capsule (for each student)

- shoebox
- craft materials for decorating
- scissors
- school glue

Additional Materials for Electrification of the U.S. activity (for each team of 3–4 students)

- whiteboard or chalkboard
- Internet access for research
- 2 pairs scissors
- 1 piece of poster board
- scotch tape or glue stick
- colored pencils
- 2 black, fine-tip pens for labeling

SAFETY NOTES

1. Remind students that personal protective equipment (safety glasses or goggles, aprons, and gloves) must be worn during the setup, hands-on, and takedown segments of activities.

2. Students should use caution when handling scissors as the sharp points and blades can cut or puncture skin.

3. Tell students to be careful when handling containers. Cut plastic may have sharp edges, which can cut or puncture skin. Plastic can break and cut skin.

CONTENT STANDARDS AND KEY VOCABULARY

Table 4.1 lists the content standards from the *Next Generation Science Standards* (NGSS), *Common Core State Standards* (CCSS), and the Framework for 21st Century Learning that this lesson addresses, and Table 4.2 presents the key vocabulary. Vocabulary terms are provided for both teacher and student use. Teachers may choose to introduce some or all of the terms to students.

Table 4.1 Content Standards Addressed in STEM Road Map Module Lesson 1

NEXT GENERATION SCIENCE STANDARDS
PERFORMANCE OBJECTIVES
• 4-ESS3-1. Obtain and combine information to describe that energy and fuels are derived from natural resources and their uses affect the environment.
• 4-PS3-2. Make observations to provide evidence that energy can be transferred from place to place by sound, light, heat, and electrical currents.
• 4-PS3–4. Apply scientific ideas to design, test, and refine a device that converts energy from one form to another.
DISCIPLINARY CORE IDEAS
ESS3.A: *Natural Resources*
• Energy and fuels that humans use are derived from natural sources, and their use affects the environment in multiple ways. Some resources are renewable over time, and others are not.
PS3.A: *Definitions of Energy*
• Energy can be moved from place to place by mobbing objects or through sound, light, or electric currents.
PS3.B: *Conservation of Energy and Energy Transfer*
• Energy is present whenever there are moving objects, sound, light, or heat. When objects collide, energy can be transferred from one object to another, thereby changing their motion. In such collisions, some energy is typically also transferred to the surrounding air; as a result, the air gets heated and sound is produced.
• Energy can also be transferred from place to place by electric currents, which can then be used locally to produce motion, sound, heat, or light. The currents may have been produced to being with by transforming the energy of motion into electrical energy.
PS3.D: *Energy in Chemical Processes and Everyday Life*
• The expression "produce energy" typically refers to the conservation of stored energy into a desired form for practical use.
CROSSCUTTING CONCEPTS
Cause and Effect
• Cause and effect relationships are routinely identified and used to explain change.
Energy and Matter
• Energy can be transferred in various ways and between objects.
Systems and System Models
• A system can be described in terms of its components and their interactions.

Table 4.1 (*continued*)

SCIENCE AND ENGINEERING PRACTICES
Asking Questions and Defining Problems
- Ask questions that can be investigated and predict reasonable outcomes based on patterns such as cause and effect relationships.

Developing and Using Models
- Develop a model to describe phenomena.
- Use a model to test interactions concerning the functioning of a natural system.

Planning and Carrying Out Investigations
- Make observations to produce data to serve as the basis for evidence for an explanation of a phenomenon or test a design solution.

Constructing Explanations and Designing Solutions
- Identify the evidence that supports particular points in an explanation.
- Use evidence (e.g., measurements, observations, patterns) to construct an explanation.
- Generate and compare multiple solutions to a problem based on how well they meet the criteria and constraints of the design solution.
- Apply scientific ideas to solve design problems.

Obtaining, Evaluating, and Communicating Information
- Obtain and combine information from books and other reliable media to explain phenomena.

COMMON CORE STATE STANDARDS FOR MATHEMATICS
MATHEMATICAL PRACTICES
- 4.MP1. Make sense of problems and persevere in solving them.
- 4.MP2. Reason abstractly and quantitatively.
- 4.MP3. Construct viable arguments and critique the reasoning of others.
- 4.MP4. Model with mathematics.
- 4.MP5. Use appropriate tools strategically.
- 4.MP6. Attend to precision.

MATHEMATICAL CONTENT
- 4.MD.A.2. Use the four operations to solve word problems involving distances, intervals of time, liquid volumes, masses of objects, and money, including problems involving simple fractions or decimals, and problems that require expressing measurements given in a larger unit in terms of a smaller unit. Represent measurement quantities using diagrams such as number line diagrams that feature a measurement scale.
- 4.MD.B.4. Make a line plot to display a data set of measurements in fractions of a unit (1/2, 1/4, 1/8). Solve problems involving addition and subtraction of fractions by using information presented in line plots.
- 4.MD.C.5. Recognize angles as geometric shapes that are formed wherever two rays share a common endpoint, and understand concepts of angle measurement.

COMMON CORE STATE STANDARDS FOR ENGLISH LANGUAGE ARTS
READING STANDARDS
- RI.4.1. Refer to details and examples in a text when explaining what the text says explicitly and when drawing inferences from the text.
- RI.4.2. Determine the main idea of a text and explain how it is supported by key details, summarize the text.
- RI.4.3. Explain events, procedures, ideas, or concepts in a historical, scientific or technical text, including what happened and why, based on specific information in the text.

Table 4.1 (*continued*)

- RI.4.4. Determine the meaning of general academic and domain-specific words or phrases in a text relevant to a grade 4 topic or subject area.
- RI.4.6. Compare and contrast a firsthand and secondhand account of the same event or topic; describe the differences in focus and the information provided.
- RI.4.7. Interpret information presented visually, orally, or quantitatively (e.g., in charts, graphs, diagrams, time lines, animations, or interactive elements on Web pages) and explain how the information contributes to an understanding of the text in which it appears.
- RI.4.9. Integrate information from two texts on the same topic in order to write or speak about the subject knowledgeably.

WRITING STANDARDS
- W.4.2. Write informative/explanatory texts to examine a topic and convey ideas and information clearly.
- W.4.6. With some guidance and support from adults, use technology, including the Internet, to produce and publish writing as well as to interact and collaborate with others; demonstrate sufficient command of keyboarding skills to type a minimum of one page in a single sitting.
- W.4.7. Conduct short research projects that build knowledge through investigation of different aspects of a topic.
- W.4.8. Recall relevant information from experiences or gather relevant information from print and digital sources; take notes and categorize information, and provide a list of sources.
- W.4.9. Draw evidence from literary or informational texts to support analysis, reflection, and research.

SPEAKING AND LISTENING STANDARDS
- SL.4.1. Engage effectively in a range of collaborative discussions (one-on-one, in groups, and teacher-led) with diverse partners on grade 4 topics and texts, building on others' ideas and expressing their own clearly.
- SL.4.4. Report on a topic or text, tell a story, or recount an experience in an organized manner, using appropriate facts and relevant, descriptive details to support main ideas or themes; speak clearly at an understandable pace.
- SL.4.5. Add audio recordings and visual displays to presentations when appropriate to enhance the development of main ideas or themes.

FRAMEWORK FOR 21ST CENTURY LEARNING
- Interdisciplinary themes (financial, economic, & business literacy; environmental literacy)
- Learning and innovation Skills
- Information, Media & Technology Skills
- Life and Career Skills

Table 4.2 Key Vocabulary in Lesson 1

Key Vocabulary	Definition
alternating current	a form of electric power in which the flow of the charge sometimes reverses direction; referred to as AC, it is used to power businesses and residences
axle	a rod that passes through the center of a wheel
biography	a true story written about a person
blade	a flat, wide section of a device, such as a propeller

Paula Schoeff et al.

Table 4.2 (*continued*)

Key Vocabulary	Definition
direct current	a form of electric power in which the flow of the charge moves in one direction only; referred to as DC, it is produced by batteries and solar cells
electrification	the process of making something work using electricity when it didn't before
energy	the ability to work; influenced by motion (kinetic energy), position (potential energy), or the mass of an object ($E=mc^2$)
force	an energy that causes motion or a change in motion
friction	a force that causes moving things to slow down when one object rubs against another object
grist mill	a building equipped with machinery that is used for grinding grain
hub	the center part of a wheel that rotates on or with the axle
hydropower	a renewable energy source for electricity that is generated by the force of moving water
kinetic energy	energy of motion
mechanical energy	the energy associated with the motion and position of an object (the sum of K.E. and P.E.)
nonrenewable	a material that is only available in limited supplies and can be used up
penstock tube	the pipe system through which water flows toward the turbine in the hydroelectric dam system
photovoltaic	a method of converting light energy into electricity using semiconductor materials
point of view	a position from which something is observed or considered; a way of thinking about a matter
potential energy	the energy that is possible due to the position of the object
renewable	a material that is never used up because it replenishes itself
run of river	a hydropower facility where water is diverted through a channel or penstock to a generating station at a lower elevation
speed	how quickly something moves
turbine	a propeller-like structure that is turned when water or air passes through it
work	when a force is applied to an object and the object is moved a distance

NATIONAL SCIENCE TEACHING ASSOCIATION

TEACHER BACKGROUND INFORMATION
Energy

One of the basic principles of physics is the law of conservation of energy. This law states that energy cannot be created or destroyed but can only be transformed to another form of energy. Classic physics also teaches that all energy exists in two basic states: potential energy, or energy due to an object's position, and kinetic energy, or the energy of motion. The work that your students do in these lessons will explore how hydroelectric dams convert the kinetic energy of falling water to electricity.

Potential energy is usually defined as the energy of position or condition. Potential energy of position can be illustrated by a ball held away from the floor. In this example, gravity pulls on the object but the object remains stationary. We say that the object has potential energy because, if released, it will immediately begin falling to earth because of gravity. Potential energy of condition can be illustrated by a common flashlight battery. The chemicals inside the battery will react and release energy whenever the negative and positive poles of the battery are connected to each other through a circuit. In the case of the ball held out over the floor, the potential energy is equal to the mass of the ball multiplied by the distance it will fall multiplied by the acceleration caused by the force of gravity. In the case of the battery, the potential energy is equal to the total energy output of the reaction until the reaction comes to a point of equilibrium.

Kinetic energy is the energy of motion. Returning to the example of the ball being held above the floor, when the ball is released, it immediately begins falling. The falling ball gains energy from gravity as it falls and its potential energy is transformed into kinetic energy. The farther the ball falls; the more kinetic energy it has. A ball dropped from a few feet has a small amount of energy and would do little damage if it were to fall on your head. The same ball falling from the top of a tall office building would have much more energy and could seriously injure someone who was struck.

Hydropower

Water always flows downhill unless pressure is used to raise it to a higher level. People have harnessed the power of falling water in the United States for hundreds of years. Conventional water wheels, such as those used in gristmills like the one described in the Millside Corners story, are powered by water falling into wooden buckets arranged around the wheel. The energy was used to turn heavy millstones used to grind wheat and corn. The amount of energy that the mill could furnish was limited by the combined weight of the water in the buckets on the water wheel and the distance that the water fell from the top of the wheel to the bottom.

Modern hydropower generating plants use the principle of falling water to convert the kinetic energy of falling water into mechanical energy in the form of spinning

turbines. The turbines spin large generators that convert rotational mechanical energy into electricity.

As in the example of the falling ball cited above, the farther the water falls, the more energy it exerts when it passes through the turbine. In hydropower systems, water is concentrated in a structure called a penstock tube. The water fills the penstock tube from deep water at the foot of the dam and flows out the end, leading into the water turbine. The total distance that the water falls is equal to the vertical distance from the surface of the water above the high end of the penstock to the bottom of the penstock.

Conventional dams have the penstock inside the dam with the turbines located near the outlet side of the dam. In this case, the penstock is restricted by the height of the dam and the amount of water that the penstock holds. In contrast, run of river (R-O-R) hydropower systems do not need a high dam to generate large amounts of power. For these, the penstock inlet may be on a fairly low dam, yet the penstock runs downhill along the river to a turbine station, sometimes for miles. This means that the vertical distance from the inlet to the turbines is not restricted by the height of the dam. Vertical distance is added by moving the bottom of the penstock tube far away downstream.

This sort of R-O-R system is one of the options for the Davis Mill hydropower project in the Millside Corners story which accompanies this lesson. In the story, the penstock tube inlet is in the dam on the Empire Creek Reservoir. The proposed penstock runs thousands of feet to the Davis Mill site, a vertical drop of nearly 25 meters. This is substantially more than could be accommodated if turbines were built in Empire Creek dam.

For more information about hydropower, see the following webpages:

- www.eia.gov/energyexplained/index.php?page=hydropower_home

- www.energy.gov/eere/water/hydropower-basics

- https://water.usgs.gov/edu/wuhy.html

Electricity in the U.S.

In the 1700s wood was burned as fuel in almost every American home and business. It was used for space heating and power generation. It was a dominant energy source because it was so easy to obtain and transport. Water powered mills and machine shops along small streams and rivers were used as well as the wind to run pumps and other simple machines. These forms of energy were reliable and abundant. Then in the 1800s, coal came on the scene and took the place of wood as an energy source.

In this lesson, students will conduct a research project and timeline activity that will help them get a sense of how energy evolved in the U.S. during the more than

200 years of the nation's existence. Students should begin to recognize that renewable energy use is not a new strategy. The first water turbine located near Niagara Falls was established in 1878, and the first electricity-generating wind turbine was brought to Cleveland Ohio by Charles Brush in 1887. Though geothermal resources have been used for more than 10,000 years, the first commercial geothermal power plant wasn't established until 1960. The discovery of photovoltaic compounds and development of solar cells paved the way for the hydrogen fuel cell used to harness electricity in Philadelphia in 1904.

Early in the 20th century electric power was largely concentrated in cities and provided by privately owned utility companies. Because of problems transmitting electricity across large distances, the gleaming lights and labor-saving electric devices of city life were missing in rural America. In the 1930s, however, President Roosevelt proposed an economic stimulus program that would bring power to rural areas and provide jobs for unemployed workers. Roosevelt's executive order established the Rural Electrification Administration (REA), which provided financial assistance to groups of farmers who agreed to build their own electrical distribution systems. This proved to be an extremely successful program.

The power grid, as we know it, began with isolated power generation systems scattered across the continent in the 1870s. The growth and unification of these systems into an interconnected alternating current (AC) power grid raised the quality of life of people from all classes. Students will discover that the first methods used to power both direct current (DC) and AC generator plants were coal-fired steam engines and hydroelectric power. As a result, most industrial cities were located near waterways that often featured dams or waterfalls. As is the case with the fictional town of Millside Corners, water powered grist mills were retrofitted into hydro-electric power generator stations. Late in the first half of the 20th century, businessmen and politicians worked to bring power to other areas that were not suitable for hydropower. Large-scale projects that brought power to rural areas were forerunners to the modern AC power three-phase power grid.

The Engineering Design Process

Students should understand that engineers need to work in groups to accomplish their work, and that collaboration is important for designing solutions to problems. Students will use the engineering design process (EDP), the same process that professional engineers use in their work, in this lesson. A graphic representation of the EDP is provided at the end of this lesson (p. XX). You may wish to provide each student with a copy of the EDP graphic or enlarge it and post it in a prominent place in your classroom for student reference throughout the module. Be prepared to review each step of the EDP with students and emphasize that the process is not a

linear one – at any point in the process, they may need to return to a previous step. The steps of the process are as follows:

1. *Define:* Describe the problem you are trying to solve, identify what materials you are able to use, and decide how much time and help you have to solve the problem.

2. *Learn:* Brainstorm solutions and conduct research to learn about the problem you are trying to solve.

3. *Plan:* Plan your work, including making sketches and dividing tasks among team members if necessary.

4. *Try:* Build a device, create a system, or complete a product.

5. *Test:* Now, test your solution. This might be done by conducting a performance test, if you have created a device to accomplish a task, or by asking for feedback from others about their solutions to the same problem.

6. *Decide.* Based on what you found out during the Test step, you can adjust your solution or make changes to your device.

After completing all six steps, students can share their solution or device with others. This represents an additional opportunity to receive feedback and make modifications based on that feedback.

The following are additional resources about the EDP:

- *www.sciencebuddies.org/engineering-design-process/engineering-design-compare-scientific-method.shtml*

- *www.pbslearningmedia.org/resource/phy03.sci.engin.design.desprocess/what-is-the-design-process*

STEM Career Connections

The Bureau of Labor Statistics' *Occupational Outlook Handbook* at www.bls.gov/ooh/home.htm provides overviews of numerous STEM careers. You may wish to introduce students to the following STEM career connections during this module (Capobianco, Parker, Laurier, & Rankin, 2015):

Civil engineer

Mechanical engineer

Environmental scientist

Geographer

Ecologist

Know, Learned, Evidence, Wonder, Scientific Principle (KLEWS) Charts

You will track student knowledge on Know, Learned, Evidence, Wonder, Scientific Principle (KLEWS) charts throughout this module. These charts will be used to access and assess student prior knowledge, encourage students to think critically about the topic under discussion, and track student learning throughout the module. Using KLEWS charts challenges students to connect evidence and scientific principles with their learning. Be sure to list the topic at the top of each chart. The charts should consist of five columns, one for each KLEWS component. It may be helpful to post these charts in a prominent place in the classroom so that students can refer to them throughout the module. Students will include their personal ideas and reflections in their STEM Research Notebooks entries. For more information about KLEWS charts, see the NSTA Books and Resources article "Evidence Helps the KLW get a KLEW" at *https://www.nsta.org/journals/science-and-children/science-and-children-february-2006/methods-and-strategies-evidence*.

COMMON MISCONCEPTIONS

Students will have various types of prior knowledge about the concepts introduced in this lesson. Table 4.3 outlines some common misconceptions students may have concerning these concepts. Because of the breadth of students' experiences, it is not possible to anticipate every misconception that students may bring as they approach this lesson. Incorrect or inaccurate prior understanding of concepts can influence student learning in the future, however, so it is important to be alert to misconceptions such as those presented in the table.

Table 4.3 Common Misconceptions about the Concepts in Lesson 1

Topic	Student Misconception	Explanation
Energy	Energy is lost, or disappears, as it is used.	Energy does not disappear but rather is transformed into other types of energy or matter.
	The power company creates energy.	Power providers provide means to transfer energy from one source, such as water at hydroelectric plants, to a form that is usable in people's homes.

PREPARATION FOR LESSON 1

Review the Teacher Background Information provided (p. XX), assemble the materials for the lesson, make copies of the student handouts, and preview the videos and slideshow recommended in the Learning Plan Components section that follows. Have your students set up their STEM Research Notebooks (see pp. XX–XX for discussion and student instruction handout). Hang chart paper and have markers on hand for creating a KLEWS chart. Be prepared to group students in teams of 3–4 students each. Students will work in these teams throughout the module.

Throughout the module, be prepared to read aloud STEM Research Notebook instructions and student handouts and check for student understanding of instructions. Review the copies of the narratives describing the problem facing the fictional town of Millside Corners. This has been provided in two formats – Teacher's Scoop on Millside Corners and Students' Scoop on Millside Corners. You will work together as a class to read the student narrative (Students' Scoop on Millside Corners). Be prepared to introduce vocabulary terms used in the narrative that students are not familiar with. You may wish to have students enter these terms and definitions in their STEM Research Notebooks. After reading the students' narratives, be prepared to provide additional geographical information from the teachers' version of the narrative (Teacher's Scoop on Millside Corners) and work as a class to sketch the site of the proposed dam that includes the geographical details provided in the narratives.

In this lesson's social studies and ELA connections, each student will choose a historical figures that they will research throughout the module. Assuming the perspective of these characters will help students to understand the issue at Millside Corners from a perspective different from their own and will therefore aid them in preparing for the debate of the question "Should Millside Corners convert Davis Mill into a hydroelectric power plant?" to be held in Lesson 4. Students will create time capsules in shoeboxes that they will add to as they learn more about their historical figure. Collect shoe boxes for each student to use to create their time capsules. Set aside a time for students to share their time capsules with the class periodically (at least twice) during the module to explain what they have learned about their historical figures. Each presentation should demonstrate that students have been reading about or researching both their primary and secondary characters to get to know them more personally and understand the topic more thoroughly. This will enable students to effectively roleplay their characters as they write blogs or create podcasts or videos.

As students research their chosen characters you may wish to employ a tiered approach in which you provide specific tasks sequentially over several weeks. The following is one example of this approach:

- **Task 1:** Identify the historical character they wish to research, then have students identify the setting in which they lived (i.e., date and location of birth, where they spent most of their lives, and date and location of death).

- **Task 2:** Identify significant contributions of the historical character they have chosen and how these contributions were received by society. Encourage students to provide additional details about the contribution that are interesting.

- **Task 3:** Ask students to find a news article or other research piece that can help them better understand the setting of their character. Students can provide examples of events occurring in that time period, an image of the clothing, or identify inventions of their character's time period. Anything that will help the students better understand their historical figure's place in history.

- **Task 4:** Who were this historical figure's contemporaries or friends? Was this person married? Did they have children? Did they have a pet? Did this they have a hobby?

- **Task 5:** Have students gather artifacts that will help them share their historical character with the class. Let the students practice writing a letter in the "voice" of their historical character to one of the characters that a peer has assumed.

Identify safe, secure, kid-friendly blog, podcasting, and video platforms for your students to prepare for the module's social studies and ELA activities, and be prepared to give students a choice of their mode of communication. Students should create one or two communication pieces (blog post, podcast, or brief video clip) per week on topics related to their learning in the module. The following are suggested topics included on the Communicating in Millside Corners student handout in Lesson 2 and may be modified as needed:

- Topic 1 – Inventions and Design

- Topic 2 – Life Around the Creek: Yesterday, Today, and Tomorrow

- Topic 3 – Electrification of Millside Corners

- Topic 4 – Does Hydropower Make Sense for Millside Corners?

- Topic 5 – Tourism around Empire Creek

- Topic 6 – Energy and the Environment

- Topic 7 – The Role of Science in Decision Making

You should decide on topics and the frequency with which students will create their blog, podcast, or video posts in advance to prepare for students to begin their postings in Lesson 2.

Compile a collection of non-fiction and fiction books about the wind or wind mills, books that can be used to compare and contrast kinetic and potential energy, books about natural resources, and biographies of the historical figures for the character study project.

You may also wish to incorporate additional literature connections into lessons. Optional literature connections include:

- *The Boy Who Harnessed the Wind* by William Kamkwanda [ISBN-13: 978–1101578636].

- *Canals and Dams: Investigate Feats of Engineering* by Donna Latham and Andrew Christensen [ISBN-13: 978–1619301658].

- *Challenging the Canyon: A Family Man Builds a Dam* by Beryl Gail Churchill [ISBN-13: 0–965294269].

LEARNING PLAN COMPONENTS
Introductory Activity/Engagement

Connection to the Challenge: Begin each day of this lesson by directing students' attention to the module challenge, the Big Changes for Millside Corners Design Challenge. Introduce the challenge by telling students that they will be challenged to create a plan to convert an existing water powered mill into a power source to convert the water in their river into electricity for use by a town called Millside Corners.

Hold a brief class discussion each day of how students' learning in the previous days' lessons contributed to their ability to complete the challenge. You may wish to create a class list of key ideas on chart paper.

Science Class and ELA Connection: Introduce the module challenge by distributing the Students' Scoop on Millside Corners handout and reading the narrative aloud as a class, introducing vocabulary terms as needed. The narrative introduces the challenge by explaining the need to convert the community mill on Empire Creek into a hydroelectric power plant. Ask students to brainstorm ideas about what they will need to know to solve this challenge and create a list of students' ideas.

Have students work as a class to make a sketch of the proposed dam site on the board on chart paper with the information provided in the Students' Scoop on Millside Corners narrative. Next, provide students with additional geographical information from the Teacher's Scoop on Millside Corners narrative. Discuss how this additional information is important in being able to visualize and sketch the site. Work as a class to add to the original sketch or create a new sketch of the dam site, labeling geographical features. Discuss how each feature in the sketch might be important for planning a solution to the module challenge.

Tell students that they will need to understand the scientific concepts associated with moving water to produce energy, and write the word *work* on the board or on chart paper, asking students to respond to the following questions:

- What comes to your mind when you hear the word "work?"

- What are some ways that work can be measured?

- How can we get work to happen?

Introduce the idea of work to the students by showing the Name that Force slideshow located at www.routledge.com/9781032618074. Explain that work occurs when force is applied to an object and it moves. Next, play the Name that Force game incorporated into the slideshow by showing students the pictures on the slideshow and asking them to identify the work being done, the force that is causing work to be done, and the source of energy that powers the force (note that answers are included in the slideshow). Have students record their ideas in their STEM Research Notebooks and then share their answers with the class before revealing the answers included in the slideshow and discussing them as a class.

Social Studies Connection: Explain to students that during the course of this module they will each roleplay as a historical figure from the past or present. Tell students that they will work in groups that have a variety of occupations and personalities represented to provide the potential for different perspectives on the challenge. Have each student choose one person from the list of historical figures provided on the Time Travelers student handout attached at the end of this lesson. After students choose their historical figures, divide students into teams of 3–4 students each so that each team includes a selection of figures from various time periods and perspectives. Have students introduce their character selections to their teams and have each team create a team name. If possible, form teams of four (the Wind Turbine EDP activity will work best with students working in pairs on their teams).

Mathematics Connection: Ask students for their ideas about how motion can be described, creating a class list of students' ideas. Next, ask students to identify items on the list that are ways to describe motion numerically. Introduce the idea to students that motion can be described by the quickness or speed of the motion, and whether the object in motion is moving increasingly quickly (acceleration) or increasingly slowly (deceleration). Introduce the idea that motion can be described not only by its speed and changes in speed, but also by the direction of the motion.

Activity/Exploration

Science Class and Mathematics Connection: Students will investigate the basic design of an air-powered turbine in the Pinwheel Activity and will build an air-powered

"turbine" from common craft items in the Wind Turbine EDP activity. The goal of the activity is to familiarize students with parts needed to create a device that can be used to convert the force of moving air or water into mechanical rotating movement.

Continue the class discussion about work and create a KLEWS chart for work, asking students to share what they know about work, how work is related to force and motion, and what they are curious about. Connect the discussion of work to the movement of air by asking students to respond to the following questions:

- One of the forces we saw in the Name that Force game was moving air; what sorts of work can be done with moving air?

- Can you give an example when moving air is used to cause changes in the direction of motion of an object?

Pinwheel Activity

In this investigation, students will work in pairs to examine a pinwheel with the goal of understanding how the components enable it to function. Distribute a pinwheel to each pair of students and a Pinwheel Activity handout to each student. Show students a pinwheel and demonstrate its motion by blowing on it or by directing a small handheld fan at it. Hold a class discussion about the pinwheel's components (axle, hub, and blades) and motion, recording students' ideas on chart paper and having students respond to the following questions in their STEM Research Notebooks:

- How could you describe the movement of the pinwheel using adverb and verb phrases?

- Does the direction of the wind flow impact a pinwheel?

- Would the direction of the wind impact the direction the pinwheel moves?

- What direction does a pinwheel turn when you blow from the front of the pinwheel? Explain your reasoning.

- What might happen when you blow from the back of the pinwheel? Explain your reasoning.

- From which direction does a wind source come to cause the pinwheel to do the most work?

Next, have each student pair make observations about their pinwheels. Ask students to describe the front view of the pinwheel both with words and with a labeled sketch. Have students describe and draw a sketch of the side view of the pinwheel on their Pinwheel Activity handouts. Students should observe that there are angled pockets in the pinwheel that catch the air to cause it to turn.

Next, have students test their predictions about the impact of air on the motion of the pinwheel by having them blow on the pinwheels from the front, back, and sides and annotating the pinwheel sketch they made previously. After students have conducted their tests, hold a class discussion, asking students for their ideas about why pinwheel responded the way that it did.

Have students record on their Pinwheel Activity handouts how their sketches show work, force, and energy.

Next, ask students if they have ever seen wind turbines. Have students look at the photograph of a wind turbine included on the last page of the Pinwheel Activity handout. Tell students that wind turbines act like supersized pinwheels and are used to convert the force of moving air into electricity. Hold a class discussion asking students to how a pinwheel is like and unlike a wind turbine, recording students' responses on chart paper.

Wind Turbine Challenge

In this activity, students are challenged to design and build an air-powered wheel using the EDP (Engineering Design Process). This device differs from the pinwheel in the direction of airflow. In the case of the pinwheel, moving air passes through from the front and causes the pinwheel to rotate sideways. The wind turbine device students will build in this activity should be designed to capture airflow from the side, so that the wheel rotates in the same direction as the flow of air. The wind turbines students build will be used in the next lesson to build a water wheel.

Introduce the EDP to students (see Teacher Background, p. XX), using the EDP graphic provided at the end of this lesson. Students should work in their teams for this activity. Hand out a set of supplies to each team and the EDP Applied to the Wind Turbine Design Challenge handout and Wind Turbine Activity handout to each student.

Teams should follow the workflow in the EDP Applied to the Wind Turbine Design Challenge handout and document their work using the Wind Turbine Activity handout. Guide students through the following steps:

Define: Teams are challenged to build a new kind of pinwheel – a wind turbine – that turns when moving air pushes on it from the side. The wheel should be able to turn freely on a stick without wobbling. The wheel should be designed to capture airflow so that the faster the air is moving, the faster the wheel will turn. The wheel should be waterproof.

Learn: Have teams inspect the materials (plastic straws, wooden stick, oak tag cards, plastic containers, modeling clay). Some students may have built similar structures using 3D building sets. Encourage them to brainstorm ideas about how to use these materials to make the wind turbine. Remind students of the

parts of the pinwheel they created (axle, hub, and fan blades) and tell them that these are also essential components of a wind turbine.

Plan: Remind students that the main sections of this device are the axle, hub, and fan blades. Instruct students to create designs for each of these sections. They should plan how each of these sections will be built and record those plans on their handouts. Students may wish to create prototypes of sections of the device as part of the planning phase.

In most cases, students will create an axle using the wooden dowel rod. Students will need to improvise a support to hold the axle. This can be something as simple as a cut out half-gallon milk jug. The hub could be, for example, a plastic straw. The center straw would serve as a bearing since it is the part of the hub in contact with the axle. There are various ways students can create fan blades, and once they have created a design they can make adjustments to the blade design to improve its performance. Students may want to prototype their fan blades with oak tag or cardboard. Once they have settled on a design, they should convert the fan blades to a waterproof material such as plastic cut from milk jugs or soda bottles.

The notes below will help you guide students through the process of building a wind turbine:

- The center straw should turn freely on the dowel rod. If it is too snug, there will be too much friction between the straw and the axle.

- The most challenging part of the structure for students will likely be the hub. Modeling clay will hold the fan blades temporarily, but since it is not rigid it will need to be replaced with something more substantial once a team has settled on a final design. The advantage of using clay is that it is easy to work with and serves well in the prototyping stage, however, the more a piece of clay is worked, the more pliable it becomes.

- This turbine prototype serves to get students thinking about how to capture the pressure of moving air or water. Flat blades may be easy to make, but they are not very efficient, particularly for water. When air or water is directed in a concentrated stream, students may find that fan blades with a slightly convex design will capture more energy.

- Rotating devices work much better if they are balanced. Students should find that a wheel with the blades distributed evenly around the hub will work better than one that is out of balance. Also, fan blades should be as identical as the students can make them. Encourage students to use a template so that all of the blades for a given prototype are the same.

- In the Wind Turbine handout, students are encouraged to create several versions of their prototype and test them with consistent criteria. Please note that the criteria given here include at least one that would not be considered performance related (color). Help students to see the difference in relevance between a criterion like color and the other examples given.

Try: Once teams have agreed on their turbine designs, have teams begin to build their turbines, using their design sketches for guidance. With a rotating device like this, it may be helpful for students to build their turbines in the following order (from the center out):

a. Create support for the axle

b. Form the hub around the center straw so the two move together

c. Build the fan blades and mount them in the hub.

Test: Hold a class discussion about how teams can test their wind turbines and collect information so that they can compare the information from the tests with another team's test results. Have students share their ideas about how they could test their turbines. Introduce the idea that taking measurements will help students rate designs in a way that provides information that can be compared with other teams' designs. Discuss examples of criteria that could be used and whether they can be measured such as:

a. Speed: how fast does the wheel turn? Revolutions per minute (RPM) is a measurement of the speed of the turbine, or how many times the fan blades revolve in one minute. Students will not be able to supply a consistent airflow by blowing for a minute. Alternatives include allowing students to test their turbines using a small handheld fan or by counting the number of revolutions as they blow consistently on the turbine for 5 seconds and then multiplying by 12. Marking one blade with a marker or using a different colored material for one of the pinwheel's blades will make it easier to count the revolutions.

b. Power: how much air does it take to turn the wheel? Have students blow through a straw to concentrate air to a steady flow. Ask them if they can measure this air flow easily and how the air flow might vary from student to student.

c. Smooth movement: does the wheel stop and start or does it turn freely? Does it wobble? Ask students if this can be easily measured.

Decide: Once teams have created working models and tested them, they should make improvements. Changing the number of fan blades and how they are shaped can change how well the model works. Remind the teams to change one thing at a

time (either blade shape or blade count) and then test their turbines so that they will know what caused the improvement.

Next, pair each team with another team and have teams give each other feedback about their designs. Provide teams with time to modify their turbines based on the feedback they receive.

Once clay used in the design has dried, it can be waterproofed with a craft sealer like Mod Podge or liquid white glue. Students should take care not to get any glue in the center straw as it could glue the turbine in place on the axle.

Social Studies and ELA Connections: Introduce the Character Study and Time Capsule activity by asking students to respond to the following questions in a class discussion:

- What is history?

- Who determines what is history and what isn't history?

- Does it matter who tells the story of history? Why or why not?

- What is meant when we say a person is a historical figure?

- Do historical figures write the history that we read in our history books?

- Are most historical events written from a first person, second person, or third person perspective?

Have students respond the following prompt in their STEM Research Notebooks:

People say we that can learn from history. Explain what this means to you.

Have students share their ideas about how people learn from history and hold a class discussion.

Character Study and Time Capsule Activity

Students will conduct research and write a short biography (at least three paragraphs) about the historical figure they chose in the Introductory Activity/ Engagement. Throughout the duration of this module they will continue to research this person and collect artifacts related to their historical figures to create time capsules (decorated shoeboxes).

Introduce this portion of the challenge by presenting the following information to students:

Time travelers and celebrities are coming to Millcreek Corners!

Professor Ipswitch is hosting his annual Millside Corners Fossil Fair. He has invited all the local townsfolk, but this is the 20th anniversary for this event so he is making it extra special by inviting your class. This will give townsfolk an opportunity to see the proposed models for Davis Mill and Empire Creek Dam for the first time.

The Professor has decided it would be exciting to hold a debate which will take place during the fair. The debate will ask the question, "Should Millside Corners convert Davis Mill into a hydroelectric power plant?" He expects the debate to be heated, so he is looking for an impartial moderator who is willing to tackle this responsibility. This moderator needs to be well informed, so the Professor is using blog, podcast, and video posts to help him make his selection. There will be two posts each week which will be used to help prepare the audience, participants, and the moderator for the big event. It should be exciting!

Instruct students to research their character, using the books you assembled and Internet research, and write a 3–5 paragraph biographical sketch of this person that includes the following information:

a. Basic facts: name, date of birth, location born and lived, why this person is famous or historically significant.

b. What makes this person interesting or special? What adjectives would best describe this person? Provide examples that illustrate those qualities.

c. What events shaped or changed this person's life? For example, did they overcome obstacles, take risks, or get lucky during their life? What effect did they have on the world or other people? Would the world be better or worse if this person had not lived? How and why?

After students conduct their research and write their biographies, have students decorate shoeboxes with images and backgrounds that are representative of the time and events that occurred when their character was alive. Explain that this will serve as a time capsule. Students will add new items to their time capsule each week to represent their character. The items students add can be images, objects, or anything else that they can use to convey information about their characters.

Explanation

Science Class and ELA and Social Studies Connections: In the Electrification of the U.S. activity, students will construct a timeline of electricity use in the U.S.

Electrification of the U.S.

Hold a class discussion to encourage students to consider the origin and source of electricity that is commonplace in the 21st century. Ask questions such as the following:

- Electricity as we experience it today has only been around since the 1800s, but this was not the first time power was utilized. Can you think of some energy sources that may have been used well before electricity was conceived?

- One hundred years ago rural communities of the U.S. did not have electricity. How would life be different if you lived in an area that didn't have electrical service?

- Electricity is important to us today. As we investigate the electrification of the U.S., you may find some surprises along the way. What do you expect was the first electrical device that was available to most households?

Discuss what the students know and want to learn about electricity and renewable and nonrenewable energy sources. Tell the students that they will research the history of electricity in the U.S. to help prepare them to address the module challenge. This activity includes three phases of activities: mapping events, sketching innovations, and drawing conclusions. The final phase, drawing conclusions, is included in the Elaboration/Application of Knowledge section of this lesson.

Phase One: Mapping events
Pass out the student handout, Electrification in the United States Timeline, to each team. Have students cut the sections apart and then work with their teams to organize the events in chronological order. Each strip includes an event and date in order to provide a baseline for students' timelines.

After students put the events in order, instruct each team to make a timeline by taping together a sheet of poster board, cut in half lengthwise. Give students time to identify and research about five additional events, in addition to the events listed on the handout. Options for additional events include:

- generators

- electric lighting

- AC and DC powered systems

- steam turbines

- centralized power stations and electric grids

- nuclear power plants

- hydropower and wind powered devices

- geothermal technologies

- non-traditional hydropower, such as wave and tidal power

Websites students may find useful include:

- Energy.gov timeline: www.energy.gov/eere/water/history-hydropower

- Energy.gov Electric Power/Energy Sources/Energy Efficiency: www.energy.gov/science-innovation/

- Electrification History: www.greatachievements.org/?id=2988; http://www.greatachievements.org/?id=2971

- How electricity grew up: A brief history of the electrical grid: www.power2switch.com/blog/how-electricity-grew-up-a-brief-history-of-the-electrical-grid/

- History of Electricity: www.instituteforenergyresearch.org/history-electricity/

- The Story of Electricity: www.storyofelectricity.org/

- Sustainable Energy in America Fact book download: https://bcse.org/market-trends/

- The History of Electrification: www.edisontechcenter.org/HistElectPowTrans.html

- History of Hydropower in the U.S.: www.usbr.gov/power/edu/history.html

- Brief History of Hydropower: www.hydropower.org/a-brief-history-of-hydropower

There should be a total of about 20 events on the timeline beginning with the 18th century or earlier through the 21st century, including at least one event in 2001 or after.

Phase Two: Sketching Inventions
Once students have put major events on the timeline, they will associate electrical devices that have been invented with these historic events. Distribute the Electrical Inventions handout to each team. Have students cut apart the strips and then research the dates of the discovery or invention. Next, have students sketch a representation of the item on the timeline where it belongs, label the sketch, and include a date for the discovery or invention.

Mathematics Connection: Hold a class discussion about speed and how it can be measured, asking questions such as:

- What is speed?

- For what kinds of things do we commonly measure speed?

- How is speed measured?

- What units do we use when we give an object's speed?

Students should understand that speed is the amount of distance an object moves in a certain amount of time.

Have students complete STEM Research Notebook entries in which they provide a definition of the term *speed* and include examples of where they have seen speed measured.

Elaboration/Application of Knowledge

Science Class and ELA and Social Studies Connections: Students will complete the third and final phase of the Electrification of the U.S. activity, drawing conclusions.

Electrification of the U.S. Phase Three: Drawing Conclusions

After teams have finished creating their timelines, have each team share their timeline of events with the class. After teams have shared their timelines, hold a class discussion about the history of electricity in the U.S., asking questions such as:

- What patterns or trends do you see on the timelines?

- Is electricity a recent discovery?

- What were some of the needs and inventions that preceded the discovery of electricity?

- How did electricity change the American way of life?

- When did the Industrial Revolution occur? (late 1700s to about 1830s)

- Did the Industrial Revolution create a need for electricity, or did electricity pave the way for an industrial boom? Are there any other trends?

If students did not discover the fact that the electrification of the U.S. began in cities in their research, tell them that many rural areas remained without electricity until about the 1930s. Additionally, students should recognize that air and water resources have been used as power sources for a long time in a primitive way, but have been utilized in a more purposeful way beginning in the 20th century.

Have each student write a reflection in their STEM Research Notebooks reflecting on the history of electricity in the U.S.

Evaluation/Assessment

Students may be assessed on the following performance tasks and other measures listed.

Performance Tasks

- Name that Force game
- Pinwheel Activity
- Wind Turbine Design Challenge
- Electrification of the U.S. Research and Timeline
- Biographical essay of a historical figure.

Other Measures

- Teacher observations
- STEM Research Notebook entries
- Student participation in teams.

INTERNET RESOURCES

Slideshow: Name that Force

- www.routledge.com/9781032618074

Hydropower resources

- www.eia.gov/energyexplained/index.php?page=hydropower_home
- www.energy.gov/eere/water/hydropower-basics
- https://water.usgs.gov/edu/wuhy.html

EDP resources

- *www.sciencebuddies.org/engineering-design-process/engineering-design-compare-scientific-method.shtml*; www.pbslearningmedia.org/resource/phy03.sci.engin.design.desprocess/what-is-the-design-process
- Bureau of Labor Statistics' *Occupational Outlook Handbook*: www.bls.gov/ooh/home.htm
- "Evidence Helps the KLW get a KLEW": *https://www.nsta.org/journals/science-and-children/science-and-children-february-2006/methods-and-strategies-evidence*

Resources for Electrification of U.S. timeline

- www.energy.gov/eere/water/history-hydropower
- www.energy.gov/science-innovation/

- www.greatachievements.org/?id=2988; http://www.greatachievements.org/?id=2971

- www.power2switch.com/blog/how-electricity-grew-up-a-brief-history-of-the-electrical-grid/

- www.instituteforenergyresearch.org/history-electricity/

- www.storyofelectricity.org/

- *https://bcse.org/market-trends/*

- www.edisontechcenter.org/HistElectPowTrans.html

- www.usbr.gov/power/edu/history.html

- www.hydropower.org/a-brief-history-of-hydropower.

BIG CHANGES FOR MILLSIDE CORNERS
TEACHER'S SCOOP ON MILLSIDE CORNERS

This is a story about a fictional small town in southern Ohio. The town serves as the setting for the module design challenge. The story revolves around an old gristmill that was converted to a hydropower plant in the early 1900s. The mill provided electricity for the town for 20 years, but fell into disuse when a large power utility extended its power grid into the area. In the story, townspeople face a decision regarding renovating the mill and nearby dam for hydroelectric power generation.

Millside Corners

Millside Corners is a pretty little town in southern Ohio. It is located in hilly country about 40 miles north of the Ohio River. The Empire Creek runs through the eastern part of town and is the site of a historic gristmill built by Hiram Davis, one of the town's founders. The town lies west of Empire Reservoir. The reservoir was created in the late 1940s when a dam was built for flood control on the Empire Creek.

Empire Creek runs year round, and the flow of water is steady because of the reservoir located upstream. The town is built into a series of long hills which slope down toward the Little Florida River. The altitude of the creek descends approximately 80 feet from the surface of the reservoir to the location of Davis Mill. Old Mill Road runs alongside the creek on the east side. Just to the east of Old Mill Road is an old railroad track that is no longer used.

Millside Corners is home to 1,500 permanent residents. Because of its location in a scenic part of Ohio, the population swells to about 2,500 in late summer and fall. Many of the temporary residents are artists and writers who come to Millside Corners to enjoy the small town atmosphere and several annual festivals. In addition to two art convocations and a bluegrass music festival, Millside Corners is home to the annual Fossil Fair held late in August. Fossil hunters converge on this region in search of Upper Ordovician fossils such as trilobites, brachiopods, corals, and shells of all kinds.

Davis Mill

Davis Mill was built in 1835 by Hiram Davis. The mill was one of several area water powered gristmills built as settlers spread east into the Ohio Valley. In those days, the Ohio River served as a major transportation artery of the fledgling United States, connecting the populous East Coast states to areas lying along the Ohio and Mississippi rivers. Farmers in the fertile valleys north and east of Millside Corners brought corn, wheat, and barley to the mill. They found ready markets for their meal, flour, and animal feed along the route served by the Ohio River corridors.

Paula Schoeff et al.

In the late 1800s, the use of electricity was spreading throughout America. In cities and towns across America, entrepreneurs were setting up electric companies and supplying power to the residents of large and medium-sized towns. In 1920, the owners of Davis Mill decided to convert the gristmill to a hydroelectric generating plant. The mill supplied power to Millside Corners for 20 years, but in the 1930s, large state-operated power companies were formed and the Davis Mill operation went out of business because it could not compete with big utilities. Twenty years later, heirs of the mill donated the mill and property along ten miles of Empire Creek to the city of Millside Corners for use as a community historical and recreational resource.

In 1961, the Davis Mill Historical Society worked to rehabilitate the mill as part of a citywide program to attract tourism and business to the area. The mill was one of the highlights of the area and hosted daily tours of the restored facilities. The mill was never restored to its original condition as a water-powered gristmill. Instead, the electrical generating apparatus supplied power for a small milling machine that produced souvenir bags of cornmeal and buckwheat flour.

The Future of Davis Mill

In recent years, with the interest in renewable energy sources, Millside Corners was the site of a study by Buckeye University students interested in small-scale hydro-power projects. Davis Mill was deemed feasible for a hydropower generator in the 2,500 to 10,000 kW class. If modernized, the Davis facility could serve as a run-of-river type of hydropower plant providing the community was willing to use public land and provide investment money. The study estimated that modernizing the hydropower plant and coupling the mill to the reservoir would cost $5M, but that substantial federal money was available for the project. The community of Millside Corners must decide whether Empire Reservoir will be used for on-the-grid hydro-power and if the generators should be located at Davis Mill or at the dam. If the town approves a hydropower plant, Millside Corners would receive money for power generated, and electricity in the area would be cheaper.

If the generators are located at the dam, the dam will need to be raised to provide adequate pressure. This will cause the reservoir to expand and cover farmland and park habitats. In addition, raising the dam would cost substantially more than retrofitting Davis Mill. If, as the Buckeye University study recommended, generators are located at Davis Mill, the mill would no longer be historical, and people would not be able to tour the mill. In both cases, there would be loss of habitat, but most of the land along the creek would still be natural. Empire Creek would continue to flow as before. If the generators are located at Davis Mill, water in the creek would no longer pass through the mill since modern generators use turbines instead of water wheels. Since the creek no longer passes through the mill wheel, the creek could be opened up for recreation such as white water rafting, kayaking, and tubing.

BIG CHANGES FOR MILLSIDE CORNERS
STUDENTS' SCOOP ON MILLSIDE CORNERS

Millside Corners

Millside Corners is a pretty little town in southern Ohio. It is located in hilly country near the Ohio River. A small river named Empire Creek runs through the edge of town. There is an old grain mill on Empire Creek that was built nearly 200 years ago. Empire Creek runs year round, and the flow of water is steady because of the reservoir located upstream. Millside Corners is built on several hills and the uphill edge of town is 80 feet higher than the part of town where Davis Mill is located.

About 1,500 people live in Millside Corners, but it is located in a very scenic part of southern Ohio. Many artists, craftsmen, and writers come to Millside Corners in the summer to enjoy the small town atmosphere and several annual festivals. In addition to two art exhibitions and a bluegrass music festival, Millside Corners is home to the annual Fossil Fair held in late August. During the weeks around the Fossil Fair, fossil hunters come from all over the country to hunt for fossils along Empire Creek and in the hills around town.

Davis Mill

Davis Mill was built in 1835 by Hiram Davis. The mill was originally a water-powered grain mill and used by farmers for nearly 100 years. In the late 1800s, the use of electricity was spreading throughout America. In cities and towns across America, power companies were built to supply electricity for homes, and businesses. In 1920, the owners of Davis Mill converted the mill to a hydroelectric power generating plant. Davis Mill supplied electricity for Millside Corners for nearly 20 years. In the 1930s, large state-operated power companies were formed and the Davis Mill operation went out of business. Several years later, the owners of Davis Mill donated the mill and property along Empire Creek to the city of Millside Corners to be used as a community historical and recreational resource.

In 1961, the historical society worked to rebuild the mill as part of a program to attract visitors and businesses to the area. The mill was one of the highlights of the area and conducted daily tours of the restored facilities. The mill was never restored to its original condition as a water-powered grain mill. Instead, the electrical generator supplied power for a machine that produced souvenir bags of cornmeal and buckwheat flour.

Paula Schoeff et al.

The Future of Davis Mill

Recently, people in the United States have become interested in renewable energy sources. Millside Corners was studied by Buckeye University students interested in new hydropower projects. The researchers determined that Davis Mill could be used as a hydropower site once again. The generator would need to be replaced and a large pipeline built from the reservoir to the mill. The study estimated that modernizing the hydropower plant and connecting it to the reservoir would cost $5 million, but some of the money could come from a U.S. government grant program. The community of Millside Corners must decide whether Empire Reservoir will be used for on-the-grid hydropower and if the generators should be located at Davis Mill or at the dam. If the town approves a hydropower plant, Millside Corners would receive money for power generated, and electricity in the area would be cheaper.

If the generators are located at the dam, the dam will need to be raised to provide adequate pressure. This will cause the reservoir to expand and cover farmland and park habitats. If generators are located at Davis Mill, the mill would no longer be historical, and people would not be able to tour the mill. In both cases, there would be loss of habitat, but most of the land along the creek would still be natural. Empire Creek would continue to flow as before. If the generators are located at Davis Mill, water in the creek would no longer pass through the mill since modern generators use turbines instead of water wheels. Since the creek no longer passes through the mill wheel, the creek could be used for recreation such as white water rafting, kayaking, and tubing.

PINWHEEL ACTIVITY

Name _____ **Date** _____

In this investigation, you will examine a pinwheel to understand how the parts allow it to function.

Examine the pinwheel at rest, and then blow on the pinwheel to make the blades move.

1. How would you describe the movement of the pinwheel?

   _____

2. In what direction does it turn? _____

3. Why do you think it is turning in this direction? _____

   _____
   _____
   _____

4. Is there a difference in motion if the air comes from the front or the back?

   _____

   Explain your reasoning. _____

   _____
   _____

5. Sketch a front and side view of the pinwheel. Identify and label the parts of the pinwheel. Indicate the direction of rotation on the front view.

Front View

Paula Schoeff et al.

PINWHEEL ACTIVITY

6. Sketch a side view of the pinwheel. Identify and label the parts of the pinwheel. Indicate the direction of rotation on the side view.

Side View

7. Describe how the sketches illustrate

   a) work: _____
      _____
      _____

   b) force: _____
      _____
      _____

   c) energy: _____
      _____
      _____

4

STUDENT HANDOUT, PAGE 3 OF 4

PINWHEEL ACTIVITY

Supersize the Pinwheel!

8. Below is a photograph of a wind turbine that is used to convert the force of moving air into electricity. How is the wind turbine like the pinwheel? How is it different?

_____

_____

_____

_____

Figure 4.1 Wind Turbine

Figure 4.1 provided by Pandaia Projects, LLC. Used with permission.

PINWHEEL ACTIVITY

Figure 4.2 Engineering Design Process (EDP)

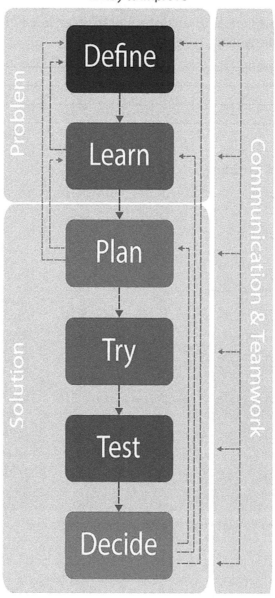

Figure 4.3 EDP Applied to the Wind Turbine Design Challenge

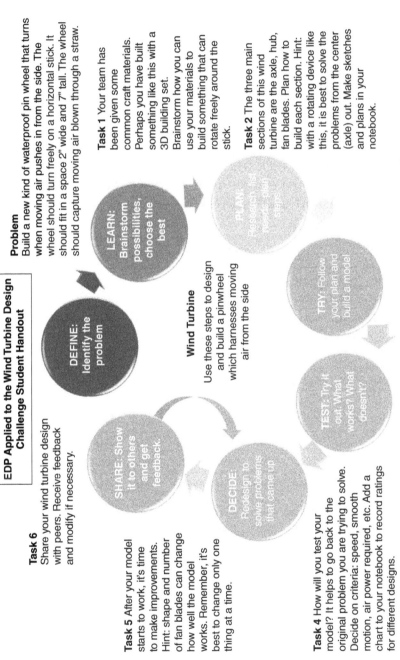

EDP Applied to the Wind Turbine Design Challenge Student Handout

Problem
Build a new kind of waterproof pin wheel that turns when moving air pushes in from the side. The wheel should turn freely on a horizontal stick. It should fit in a space 2" wide and 7" tall. The wheel should capture moving air blown through a straw.

Task 1 Your team has been given some common craft materials. Perhaps you have built something like this with a 3D building set. Brainstorm how you can use your materials to build something that can rotate freely around the stick.

Task 2 The three main sections of this wind turbine are the axle, hub, fan blades. Plan how to build each section. Hint: with a rotating device like this, it is best to solve the problems from the center (axle) out. Make sketches and plans in your notebook.

Task 3 Get to work building your model using the plan you made. Start simple: 2 or 3 fan blades. Hint: blades should be spaced evenly for balance. Add notes to your sketches as you get things working.

Wind Turbine
Use these steps to design and build a pinwheel which harnesses moving air from the side

DEFINE: Identify the problem

LEARN: Brainstorm possibilities, choose the best

PLAN

TRY: Follow your plan and build a model

TEST: Try it out. What works? What doesn't?

DECIDE: Redesign to solve problems that came up

SHARE: Show it to others and get feedback

Task 6
Share your wind turbine design with peers. Receive feedback and modify if necessary.

Task 5 After your model starts to work, it's time to make improvements. Hint: shape and number of fan blades can change how well the model works. Remember, it's best to change only one thing at a time.

Task 4 How will you test your model? It helps to go back to the original problem you are trying to solve. Decide on criteria: speed, smooth motion, air power required, etc. Add a chart to your notebook to record ratings for different designs.

4   Paula Schoeff et al.

WIND TURBINE ACTIVITY

Name _____ Date _____

In this activity, you will build a wind turbine using the EDP to solve the following challenge:

Your team is challenged to build a new kind of wind turbine that turns when moving air pushes on it from the side. Each team will have access to all the materials, but your team does not need to use all the materials provided; the materials used will vary according to each team's design.

Wind Turbine Activity Materials	
• 3/16" x 12" dowel rod • ¼" plastic straws • 2 sheets of oak tag card stock or note cards • empty plastic packaging such as milk jugs or soda bottles to be cut up as needed • masking tape • EDP Applied to the Wind Turbine Design Challenge handout • STEM Research Notebooks	• air dry modeling clay • craft sealant if paper or air dry clay used • plastic spoons • small craft straws or coffee stirrers • foil pie pan • craft sticks • large paper clips

Requirements for your turbine:

_____ 1. The turbine should be able to turn freely on a stick (dowel rod) without wobbling.

_____ 2. It should turn freely in a space 2" wide and 7" tall with the axle running through the 2" width

_____ 3. The turbine should be designed to capture air so that the faster the air is moving, the faster the turbine will turn.

_____ 4. The final version of the turbine should be waterproof.

WIND TURBINE ACTIVITY

1. Sketch front and side views showing the three main sections of the wind turbine you will build on the following page or in your STEM Research Notebook.

   - Axle

   - Hub

   - Fan Blades

Front View
Side view

Paula Schoeff et al.

WIND TURBINE ACTIVITY

2. Draw and label the materials needed to build the section.

axle and support
hub
Fan blades

3. In steps 3, 4, and 5, you build, test, and improve the model to get it working as well as possible. That means you may create different versions of the model. How will you test and measure the performance of your versions? Create a chart to record your measurements for each version of your model. If the chart on the next page is not adequate, make one of your own in your STEM research notebook. The list below has several different measurement criteria. Choose ones that make sense or add your own.

- speed (RPM): fast/medium/slow

- color: red/blue/green/yellow/other

- weight

- air power needed

- _____

WIND TURBINE ACTIVITY

Version	Design Notes	Measurements	Design Rating

4. In step 6, compare your design with one other team. Note their feedback below and note any improvements you make to your design.

Peer Feedback	Improvements

5. Once you are satisfied with your design, create a final version using waterproof material for the hub and fan blades. This will be your waterproof working model. If using air-dry clay, it will take a day or two to dry. Be sure to support the model so that the blades stay in the correct position while the hub dries.

6. If needed, coat paper and clay parts thoroughly with glue sealer such as Mod Podge, and set the assembly aside to dry thoroughly. Insure that no glue sealer gets in the center straw or it will glue the turbine in place on the axle.

4   Paula Schoeff et al.

BIOGRAPHICAL ESSAY AND TIME CAPSULE

The quote "you never really understand a person until you consider things from his point of view – until you climb into his skin and walk around in it" was delivered by Atticus Finch in *To Kill a Mockingbird* and means that when you hear, see, or experience other people's lives, you can consider how you would deal with a situation if you were in their position.

As you work through this module, you will take an active role in helping the citizens of Millside Corners with their big decision on the Davis Mill hydroelectric power question. This decision will have a lasting impact on Millside Corners for many years to come – perhaps forever! You will work through this decision as a time traveler who has come to visit Millside Corners. Review the list of time travelers and think about who you would like to spend the next few weeks getting to know. You will do some research on the person and "walk in his skin" as you roleplay the character while creating blog, podcast, or video posts.

Your social studies grade for participating in this project will be based on the following:

1. **Writing a biographical essay** of a historical figure. This should be a 3–5 paragraph essay that includes the following:

   a) Basic facts: name, date of birth, location born and lived, why this person is famous, etc.

   b) What makes this person interesting or special? What adjectives would best describe this person, provide examples that illustrate those qualities?

   c) What events shaped or changed this person's life? Did they overcome obstacles, take risks, or get lucky during their life? What effect did they have on the world or other people? Would the world be better or worse if this person had not lived? How and why?

NOTE: You will need to know major historical events that are taking place at the time your person was alive, as well as events in this person's life. For example, you cannot understand Abraham Lincoln without knowing something about the American Civil War. Historical events are very

(continued)

BIOGRAPHICAL ESSAY AND TIME CAPSULE

important influences on the way people think and feel – and may have an impact on your character's beliefs about the Millside Corner hydropower project.

2. **Create a time capsule:** Decorate a shoe box to serve as a time capsule.

3. You will **add objects** that reflect the life and times of your historical figure inside the time capsule over the course of the module.

4. You will communicate with your fellow time travelers 2–3 times a week. Your teacher will let you know how this will be done. Be sure to reference the research you have done. Extra points will be awarded when you provide new information!

4   Paula Schoeff et al.

HISTORICAL FIGURES

Look over the list of historical figures and choose one who interests you. You will spend the next few weeks getting to know this person through research. Your research will help you roleplay this person as they come to Millside Corners and become interested in the big changes that are coming.

Inventors	Engineers
Michael Faraday: invented the first electric generator **Ada Lovelace:** British mathematician who is considered the world's first computer programmer **Orville Wright:** American inventor and businessman who, with his brother Wilbur Wright, built the first airplane to fly under its own power **Ben Franklin:** American statesman, scientist, and inventor who pioneered the study of electricity **Margaret Knight:** American computer scientist who developed ways to simplify complicated computer programs **Thomas Edison:** American inventor and businessman who is credited with many inventions associated with the modern age **George Westinghouse, Jr:** American engineer and entrepreneur whose ideas for electricity distribution led to the modern power grid	**Frank Galbraith:** American self-taught engineer who developed ways to simplify factory work as a method for improving quality **Henry Ford:** American inventor and industrialist who founded the Ford Motor Company and pioneered use of the assembly line method of manufacturing **Bernard Forest deBelidor:** French engineer who developed the science of hydraulics and built the first turbine **Burt Rutan:** American aerospace engineer who developed ways to make airplanes and spacecraft lighter and more fuel efficient **Melitta Bentz:** German entrepreneur who designed and invented the first coffee filter **Katharine Burr Blodgett:** American scientist who invented special coatings for glass **Hedy Lamarr:** American actress who invented radio technology used in weapons guidance, Wi-Fi, and Bluetooth
Artists/Writers	Naturalists
Leonardo da Vinci: Italian artist and scientist who pioneered new forms of painting and mechanics **Walt Disney:** American entrepreneur, animator, and film producer **J. K. Rowling:** British novelist famous for the Harry Potter series of young adult novels **C. S. Lewis:** British novelist, philosopher, and essayist famous for his books about a fantasy land called Narnia **Pablo Picasso:** Spanish painter and sculptor famous for introducing a new style of art in the mid-20th century **Angelina Jolie:** American actress and humanitarian working with Afghan refugees, conservation efforts, and child immigration	**Rachel Carson:** writer who opened the eyes of U.S. politicians to the evils of pollution and pesticides **John Chapman** (Johnny Appleseed): a skilled nurseryman **Carol Dormon:** a naturalist who work in many parks and helped develop the first arboretum **John James Audubon:** bird scientist and artist **Florence Merriam:** bird scientist, began a science called ornithology **Enos Mills:** father of Rocky Mountain National Park **John Muir:** father of national parks **Henry David Thoreau:** naturalist, essayist, poet **Freeman Tilden:** paved the way for "interpreting nature" to make it meaningful

HISTORICAL FIGURES

Business Men and Women	Scientists
John D. Rockefeller: American businessman who co-founded the Standard Oil Company **William Randolph Hurst:** American newspaper publisher who founded America's largest newspaper chain **Madam C. J. Walker:** American entrepreneur and philanthropist; born into poverty and became the first Black woman millionaire in the United States **Marissa Mayer:** American software engineer who serves as CEO of Yahoo **Mark Zuckerberg:** American software engineer who founded and leads Facebook **Bill Gates:** American programmer who co-founded Microsoft and leads the Bill and Melinda Gates Foundation **Warren Buffett:** American business leader widely regarded as the most successful investor of the 20th century **Steve Jobs:** American businessman who co-founded Apple and served as the CEO of Pixar **Jeff Bezos:** American businessman who founded and serves as the CEO of Amazon **Indra Nooyi:** India-born, naturalized American businesswoman who serves as the CEO of PepsiCo	**Albert Einstein:** German scientist who developed the theory of relativity. **Stephen Hawking:** British scientist who developed new ideas about space **Robert Oppenheimer:** American scientist who led the development of atomic power **Jonas Salk:** American medical researcher who developed a vaccine to prevent polio, a terrible disease **Bill Nye:** American science educator who produced a children's science television show **Marie Curie:** French scientist who developed the theory of radioactivity **Nina Tandon:** American founder of a company that uses stem cells to grow human bones **Cynthia Kenyon:** American molecular biologist who is developing ways to help us live longer **Katalin Karikó:** Hungarian-born American chemist whose research laid the groundwork for the mRNA vaccine, allowing development of the COVID-19 vaccines and who won the Nobel Prize for this work

4   Paula Schoeff et al.

HISTORICAL FIGURES

Male Political Figures	Female Political Figures
Bill Clinton: 42nd President of the United States who presided over the longest period of peacetime economic growth in American history **Abdul Kalam:** 11th President of India who, as a scientist, helped launch India's space program **Nelson Mandela:** South African president who led the fight for freedom and equal rights for blacks in South Africa **John F. Kennedy:** American president who launched the American Space Program **Martin Luther King, Jr:** American Baptist minister who led the fight for civil rights in the United States during the 1960s	**Princess Catherine (Duchess of Cambridge):** British woman married to Prince William, Duke of Cambridge **Hillary Clinton:** American politician who has served as first Lady of the United States, U.S. Senator, and Secretary of State **Angela Merkel:** First woman Chancellor of Germany **Emmeline Pankhurst:** British political leader of the women's suffrage movement **Maya Angelou:** American poet, historian, and civil rights activist **Abigail Adams:** Wrote about her life and time in letters and exerted political influence over her president husband, John Adams
Other Great Men	Other Great Women
Pope Francis: Argentinian priest chosen as the 266th Pope of the Catholic Church **Edson Arantes do Nascimento (Pele):** Brazilian soccer player widely regarded as the greatest player of all time **Scott Harrison:** American CEO of Charity Water, an organization that works to provide clean drinking water to impoverished people **Paul McCartney:** British musician who wrote 32 songs as a member of the Beatles and as a solo performer **Bono:** Irish musician who leads the rock group U2 and serves as spokesman for many charities **Carl Sagan:** American astronomer who produced a popular television show about space **Patrick Moore:** British amateur astronomer who hosted a popular BBC television show about space	**Mother Theresa:** Roman Catholic nun and missionary famous for her work with the poor in Calcutta, India **Amelia Earhart:** American aviator who became the first woman to fly solo across the Atlantic Ocean **Billie Jean King:** American professional tennis player who crusaded for equal opportunities for female athletes **Millicent Fawcett:** British feminist and crusader for women's access to higher education **Wendy Kopp:** American educator and founder of Teach for America **Oprah Winfrey:** American television personality widely regarded as the most influential woman in the world

ELECTRIFICATION OF THE U.S. PROJECT DESCRIPTION

Most of us take electricity for granted. We wake up in the morning with a clock radio alarm, turn on the lights to get dressed, and perhaps turn on the radio or television as we finish getting ready. We get milk out of the refrigerator for oatmeal we cook on the electric range or in the microwave oven. Yet without power plants, thousands of miles of wire, and constant monitoring of the electric power grid, our electricity would not exist – nor would the modern world as we know it. Without electricity to power factories we wouldn't have automobiles, nor would we have the miles of roadways and highways that stretch across our country or the traffic lights and street lamps that brighten our sidewalks at night. Tall buildings would be impractical because powerful, lightweight electric motors move elevators up to and down from floors high above the street. In fact, it is hard to imagine our world without the widespread electrification that occurred in the 20th century, not only in the U.S., but also in all the world's industrialized nations.

The story of electrification in the U.S. has been dependent upon both public and private investments and has relied on the innovative engineers who dared to "think outside the box." Early in the century, the distribution of electric power was primarily concentrated in cities, beginning with Thomas Edison's power plant in 1882. It wasn't until President Roosevelt's executive order to establish the Rural Electrification Administration in 1935 that country towns were able to take advantage of the electrification advances.

Procedure: Timeline

1. Begin your research by reading through the list of items on the Electrification of the United States handout as you cut them out and put them in chronological order on your desk.

2. After you have these in order, cut a piece of poster board in half longways, tape the ends together, and use a ruler to create a timeline from 1700 to today. Leave room below the line for adding events and above the line for the inventions you will add later.

3. Select up to 15 events from the handout for your timeline. Add five new events that occurred during the electrification of the United States using one of the websites provided below as a resource. You should have 20 events when you finish your timeline. These events should span from the 18th century (1800 or before) through the 21st century (2000 and beyond).

4   Paula Schoeff et al.

ELECTRIFICATION OF THE U.S. PROJECT DESCRIPTION

As you research, select 7 electrical inventions to add using the inventions from the handout or other inventions you discovered in your research. When adding inventions, draw a picture with a line that leads to the proper location on the timeline.

Sources for Research

- Energy.gov timeline: www.energy.gov/eere/water/history-hydropower

- Energy.gov Electric Power/Energy Sources/Energy Efficiency: www.energy.gov/science-innovation/

- Electrification History: www.greatachievements.org/?id=2988; http://www.greatachievements.org/?id=2971

- How electricity grew up: www.power2switch.com/blog/how-electricity-grew-up-a-brief-history-of-the-electrical-grid/

- History of Electricity: www.instituteforenergyresearch.org/history-electricity/

- The Story of Electricity: www.storyofelectricity.org/

- Sustainable Energy in America Fact book download: https://bcse.org/market-trends/

- The History of Electrification: www.edisontechcenter.org/HistElectPowTrans.html

- History of Hydropower in the U.S.: *www.usbr.gov/power/edu/history.html*

- Brief History of Hydropower: www.hydropower.org/a-brief-history-of-hydropower

STUDENT HANDOUT, PAGE 1 OF 3

ELECTRIFICATION OF THE UNITED STATES TIMELINE

In 1769 Boulton & Watt patented the modern day **steam engine**. It met the demands of the paper mill, coal mines, and iron mills during the Industrial Age.

The first known commercial use of **geothermal energy** was established in Hot Springs, Arkansas (1892) when Asa Thompson began charging for the use of the spring-fed baths.

The inventor Thomas Alva Edison experimented with thousands of different filaments to find just the right materials to glow well and be long lasting. In 1879, Edison invented a carbon filament in a **lightbulb** that glowed for 40 hours.

In 1893 **alternating current (AC)** was introduced to the world when Nikola Tesla, a Westinghouse Electric Co. engineer, powered the World's Fair in Chicago. This event fueled the "War of the Currents" between Tesla and Edison.

The first **personal computers**, introduced in 1975, surprisingly were not produced by IBM or Microsoft; instead, they were kits that were ordered through the mail. This is the same year that the first **video game** PONG was created for the Atari®.

In 1935, Morris Llewellyn Cooke, a mechanical engineer, devised a **rural distribution system** for power companies in New York and Pennsylvania which was adopted by Franklin Delano Roosevelt to electrify rural areas of the United States.

Thousands came to Black Canyon (Nevada) during the Depression (1936) to tame the Colorado River by building the world's largest hydroelectric dam of its time, the **Hoover Dam.**

The high costs in World War II (1945) brought about innovations with nuclear energy to develop a civilian nuclear power industry. The prime focus has been to produce reliable **nuclear power plants**.

In 1876. Adams and Day discovered that selenium produced electricity when exposed to light. This proved that light, without heat or moving parts, could be converted into electricity. This was an introduction to **solar cells.**

Structures began being built near geysers to take advantage of the natural heat of these geothermal landforms. In 1864 Newhard built the first large-scale project, the **Hot Lake Hotel complex**, in Oregon to utilize geothermal energy.

ELECTRIFICATION OF THE UNITED STATES TIMELINE

Townes and Schawlow disproved many skeptics in 1958 by creating a **laser** which bounced light back and forth to create radio waves that is used for CD players, corrective eye surgery, tattoo removal, supermarket scanners, and much more.

The first **hydroelectric power plant** in the U.S. was built at Niagara Falls in 1879. The gravity caused the water to fall into a reservoir, and the force from the falling water was used to turn a turbine and generate electricity.

In 1917, American Gas & Electric established the first **long-distance high-voltage transmission power line**. The power plant from which the line ran was the first major steam plant to be built at the mouth of the coal mine that supplied its fuel.

In 1922, John Grant helped establish the United States' first geothermal plant at **The Geysers**. The Geysers is the world's largest geothermal field, spanning an area of nearly 30 square miles.

Water wheels were used to power factory machinery, such as the big saws in lumber mills in the 1800s. Water wheels were displaced by the smaller, more efficient **turbine** developed in 1827 which was not as dependent on flowing water.

The **Drake Well** in Pennsylvania was the first oil well established with the intent to tap into the oil reserve underground. Before 1859, most wells were drilled for salt brine and produced oil as an accidental byproduct.

A public electric utility industry was launched in 1882 when Edison created a DC electric power system at the **Pearl Street Station** to power Manhattan's electric lights which used the new Edison light bulb.

The first **wind-powered turbine** to generate electricity was a backyard 60-ft structure that powered 408 batteries in the basement of Charles Brush's mansion in Cleveland, OH. (1887)

After nuclear fission was used during World War II, a great deal of research into atomic energy was done. The first usable electricity from a nuclear fission reaction was produced in 1953 at the **National Reactor Station** in Idaho.

The roof on the **Bridgers-Paxton office building** had a 30-degree slant to capture the intense heat of New Mexico's sun rays. Its 1956 construction as the world's first solar-heated office building was revolutionary.

Folks in Boise, Idaho, felt the heat of the world's first district **geothermal heating system** in 1892 when water was piped from a nearby hot springs into town buildings.

ELECTRIFICATION OF THE UNITED STATES TIMELINE

The Grand Rapids Muskegon Power Co. built the **Croton Hydroelectric Plant** in 1907. Curious engineers from all over the world came to ride a train to the site and receive a tour of the dam and powerhouse.
Two German scientists and a physicist in Austria worked together in 1938 to discover that when the nucleus of a uranium atom is split some of its mass is converted into heat energy (this is called **nuclear fission**).
The earliest hydroelectric power plant was built in Grand Rapids, Michigan (1880), where the water turbine at the **Wolverine Chair factory** was attached to a dynamo and used a belt drive to employ a DC current to light 16 street lamps.

Paula Schoeff et al.

ELECTRICAL INVENTIONS

Many inventions have impacted the history of electricity in the U.S. Some inventions, such as the first water wheel, were not used to generate power. Water wheels were, however, instrumental in the design of future wheels and turbines, which were used to provide power.

radio alarm clock	color television	CD player
battery	electric typewriter	first water wheel (for power)
microwave oven	first (verified) windmill used for power	moving pictures (movies)
wireless radio (CB)	hybrid gasoline-electric car	electric guitar
phonograph	solar backpack	cell phone

STEM RESEARCH NOTEBOOK RUBRIC

Name: _____   Score:_____

10	**Exceeds Expectations**
	• The writing goes beyond the basic requirements and shows in-depth understanding of concepts.
	• The work shows in-depth reflection throughout the learning process.
	• The notebook has all the components expected, including dates and labels on each page.
	• All pages are numbered properly, with odd numbers on the right and even numbers on the left.
	• Work is correctly organized, with all criteria.
	• The use of color and labeled diagrams enhances understanding.
	• The notebook is very neat.
9	**Meets Expectations**
	• The writing follows the basic requirements and shows understanding of concepts, but does not go beyond.
	• The work shows in-depth reflection.
	• The notebook has all the components expected, including dates and labels on each page.
	• All pages are numbered properly, with odd numbers on the right and even numbers on the left.
	• Work is correctly organized, with all criteria.
	• The notebook has color and uses labeled diagrams.
	• The notebook looks much like one that receives a score of 10, but it lacks the perfection.
8	**Approaches Expectations**
	• The written work shows a basic understanding of concepts.
	• The work is an honest reflection, but it is limited.
	• The notebook has about 90% of the components expected, with dates and labels.
	• All pages are numbered properly, with odd numbers on the right and even numbers on the left.
	• Work is correctly organized.
	• The notebook has some color and diagrams, with a few labels.
	• Some requirements are met, but the notebook does not meet all criteria.
7	**Needs Some Improvement**
	• The written work shows a limited understanding of concepts.
	• The work shows limited reflection overall.
	• The notebook has about 80% of the components, with dates and labels.
	• Most pages are numbered.
	• Work is fairly organized but just so-so.
	• The notebook has very little color and few diagrams.
	• Notebook requirements are met inconsistently.
6	**Needs Much Improvement**
	• The written work shows misconceptions and a lack of understanding.
	• The work includes little to no reflection.
	• The pages in the notebook are unfinished.
	• There are incomplete dates and labels.
	• There are inconsistencies in right- and left-side entries.
	• The notebook is unorganized, and one or two pages are blank.
5	**Incomplete**
	• Many pages are blank or include the class templates only.

Paula Schoeff et al.

Name _____ Topic _____

COLLABORATION RUBRIC

Expectations	Exceeds Expectations (4)	Meets Expectations (3)	Approaching Expectations (2)	Needs Improvement (1)	Incomplete (0)
SELF-REFLECTION I stayed on task while working with my team.					
SELF-REFLECTION I communicated with my team and documented the work accurately.					
SELF-REFLECTION I read and followed the directions carefully.					
SELF-REFLECTION We were successful and completed the activity and I did my best.					
SELF-REFLECTION I did an equal amount of work as others on my team.					
TEACHER INPUT Student had an equal share of the responsibility and did not let their team down.					
TEACHER INPUT Student's insight benefitted the team and contributed to the team's success.					
TEACHER INPUT Student did not play around, but stayed on task and followed directions.					
Comments:					

Name _____ Topic _____

PEER REVIEW COLLABORATION RUBRIC

Expectations	Exceeds Expectations (4)	Meets Expectations (3)	Approaching Expectations (2)	Needs Improvement (1)	Incomplete (0)
PEER EVALUATION Participated equally and was an important part of our success.					
PEER EVALUATION Made good decisions which helped our team stay on task and do our best.					
PEER EVALUATION Maintained a positive attitude about the project.					
Comments:					

PINWHEEL ACTIVITY RUBRIC

Name_____

	Exceeds Expectations (4)	Meets Expectations (3)	Approaching Expectations (2)	Needs Improvement (1)	Incomplete (0)
Observations Score	• Observations are accurate & complete. • Interpretations are based on experiences and observations.	• Observations are accurate & complete. • Interpretations are based only on lab observations.	• Observations are accurate, but miss important details. • Lab did not inform interpretation.	• Observations are "on the right track." • Little or no background knowledge available.	• Nonsense or blank response. • No reflection about lab is present.
Predictions Score	• Clearly understands how the device or principle works. • Explains predictions and identifies reasoning.	• Understands how the device or principle works. • Can make reasonable predictions but does not explain reasoning.	• Grasps the principles of the device. • Cannot make predictions based on knowledge.	• Can draw conclusions about the device or principle. • Vaguely understands relationships or principles associated.	• Nonsense or blank response. • Does not have any knowledge necessary to complete this activity successfully.
Pictures Score	• Drawings are detailed. • Detailed labels and descriptions. • Labels reflect appropriate vocabulary.	• Drawings contain several details. • All the important labels & descriptions are present. • Labels reflect a growing vocabulary.	• Drawings contain some details. • Labels drawing, but leaves out some important details. • Labels include few science terms.	• Drawing is not detailed. • Labels are incorrect, confusing, or non-technical, e.g., "circle thing-y" • No science terms.	• Unfinished drawing • No labels. • No science terms.
Data and Results Score	• Tables/graphs are neat and clearly labeled. • Tables/graphs are accurate and used effectively. • Data used the best method so patterns/trends can be seen.	• Tables/graphs are labeled. • Tables/graphs are all accurate, but not helpful. • Some data is shown with the best method so that some patterns can be seen.	• Tables/graphs are mislabeled. • Tables/graphs are inaccurate and difficult to interpret. • Data is unclear so that it is not possible to make clear predictions.	• Much of the data is not recorded on the tables/graphs. • It is not possible to use the tables/graphs to find a pattern. • Incorrect corrections are made due to bad data.	• No tables/ graphs are visible. • No data is provided. • No predictions can be made.

Comments:

4

WIND TURBINE CHALLENGE RUBRIC, PAGE 1 OF 4

Name_____

(42 possible points)

DEFINE: Identify the Problem		
5–6	• Student has a clear understanding of the problem and its requirements. • Student can use other ideas, concepts, or processes to construct explanations. • Student can apply knowledge to predict and solve complex problems, including those in unfamiliar situations.	
3–4	• Student can describe the problem and its requirements. • Student can recall other ideas, concepts, or processes that are identical. • Student can apply knowledge to predict and solve complex problems in familiar situations.	
1–2	• Student needs help to understand the problem. • Student may be able to recall some ideas, concepts, or processes that are identical. • Student is able to recognize and mimic examples of other solutions to the problem.	
LEARN: Brainstorm Possibilities, Choose the Best		
5–6	• All ideas are focused on solving the problem. • Student considers unlikely solutions/models. • Student uses ideas, concepts, or processes correctly to construct possible solutions.	
3–4	• Some ideas are focused on solving the problem. • Student considers multiple solutions/models. • Student mimics (copies) the best option.	
1–2	• Few ideas are focused on solving the problem. • Student uses examples or direct guidance to generate ideas for solving the problem/developing a model. • Student does not provide any original ideas.	

Paula Schoeff et al.

WIND TURBINE CHALLENGE RUBRIC, PAGE 2 OF 4

PLAN: Research, List Needs, Plan Steps		
5–6	• Student critically investigates the problem and selects information from a broad range of sources. • Student provides a complete list of the materials needed. • Student plans and explains the steps that are used, including all of the techniques that are required.	
3–4	• Student analyzes and selects information from some recommended sources. • Student provides a list with most of the materials needed. • Student plans and explains the steps that are used with few omissions.	
1–2	• Student investigates the problem, collecting information from sources. • Student lists some of the materials needed. • Student plans and explains few of the steps that are needed.	
TRY: Follow Your Plan and Build a Model		
5–6	• Student provides detailed drawings which provide valuable information for constructing the model. • Student provides a comprehensive list of criteria for success and reasonable methods for testing each one. • Student generates a range of feasible solutions and justifies the chosen prototype.	
3–4	• Student provides drawings that provide enough information to construct a model. • Student provides some criteria for success and reasonable methods for testing them. • Student generates an alternate solution if something doesn't work right.	
1–2	• Student provides rough sketches of the design which are not very helpful. • Student provides no criteria for success or a method for testing them. • Student generates one solution (even if a better alternative becomes available).	

WIND TURBINE CHALLENGE RUBRIC, PAGE 3 OF 4

TEST: Try It Out! What Works? What Doesn't?	
5–6	• Student is able to manipulate materials and equipment with skill. • Student consistently adheres to plans in a precise and methodical manner. • Comprehensive testing has been done to assess the performance of the model/solution. • Test results are well documented and conclusive.
3–4	• Student is able to manipulate materials and equipment to complete the task. • Student carries out the plan but overlooks some aspects. • The model/solution is tested against a minimum set of standards for success. • Test results are well documented and reasonable.
1–2	• Student is not able to manipulate equipment and materials satisfactorily. • Student has not followed the specified instructions outlined in the plan. • Student has not tested the model/solution adequately. • Test results are inconclusive or misleading.
DECIDE: Redesign to Solve Problems That Come Up	
5–6	• Student's evaluation is a thoughtful and insightful assessment based on the performance against a complete set of defined criteria for success. • The evaluation statements are justified and supported with evidence, taking into account the effectiveness and efficiency. • Realistic and innovative suggestions are made for improvement of the model/solution.
3–4	• Student's evaluations are justified and supported with evidence taking effectiveness and efficiency of the solution/model into consideration. • Student measures performance against most of the defined criteria for success. • Student provides some realistic suggestions to address the problem or improve performance.
1–2	• Student states expected performance. • Student considers only one or two of the defined criteria for success for the solution/model. • Little or no attention was given to the effectiveness or efficiency of the performance of the model/solution.

Paula Schoeff et al.

WIND TURBINE CHALLENGE RUBRIC, PAGE 4 OF 4

SHARE: Show It to Others and Get Feedback		
5–6	• Student received feedback from peers with a variety of backgrounds and with other experiences to improve design. • Student sought feedback from a parent or teacher to get feedback on design. • Student analyzed and implemented indicated improvements.	
3–4	• Student received feedback from several friends who they associate with regularly to improve design. • Student has not sought feedback from experts. • Considered but did not implement indicated improvements.	
1–2	• Student received feedback from a peer. • Student has not sought feedback from any other person. • Considered the current prototype good enough.	
Comments: 		

Remember, there is no one "right" answer – many solutions/models are possible.

4

BIOGRAPHY RUBRIC

Name _____   Score_____

	Exceeds Expectations (4)	Meets Expectations (3)	Approaching Expectations (2)	Needs Improvement (1)	Incomplete (0)	Score
USE OF HISTORICAL FIGURE (CHARACTER)	Written like a pro! The character's voice is used and life events are mentioned. Their personality shines through!	Written VERY well! The character's voice is used and life events are mentioned. Their personality is being revealed.	Writing is acceptable. Events from the character's life are mentioned with a peek at their personality once in a while.	Poor construction. Events in the character's life are mentioned briefly with no attempt to bring out their personality.	Not satisfactory. The character is not a focal point of the writing.	
FLOW OF EVENTS	Paragraphs are clear and in a logical order.	Paragraphs are clear and in a logical order.	Paragraphs are not clear and are difficult to follow.	Paragraphs are not a single topic and story is difficult to follow.	It is incomplete and does not follow the required structure.	
CONTENT 1	Demonstrates thorough knowledge of chosen person's life and provides many details.	Demonstrates a good knowledge of chosen person's life and provides some details.	Adequate knowledge of the character's life and provides few details.	Some knowledge of their chosen person's life, but provides only one or two details.	Very little or no knowledge of chosen person's life is revealed.	
CONTENT 2	Uses many descriptive adjectives to provide insight. Examples help explain why these adjectives were chosen.	Uses few descriptive adjectives to provide insight. Examples are used to help explain.	Uses several descriptive adjectives. Does not provide examples to explain why these adjectives were chosen.	Uses a few descriptive adjectives. Does not provide examples to explain why these adjectives were chosen.	Provides neither adjectives to give insight into this person's character nor an explanation.	
CONTENT 3	Two or more events are important to the person & community.	Tells how two events are important to the person OR community.	Tells how one event is important to the person & community.	Tells how one event is important to the person OR community.	Identifies events, but does not explain why they are important.	
ACCURACY	All facts about the person, turning points, and accomplishments are accurate.	Most facts about the person, turning points, and accomplishments are accurate.	Some facts about the person, turning points, and accomplishments are accurate.	Few facts about the person, turning points, and accomplishments are accurate.	Facts about the person, turning points, and accomplishments are not accurate.	
LANGUAGE and GRAMMAR	Punctuation and grammar make the story easier to read. No errors.	Punctuation and grammar make story easier to read. Few errors.	Punctuation and grammar errors do not affect the meaning.	Frequent errors in punctuation and grammar make it difficult to understand.	Punctuation and grammar errors change the meaning.	
RESEARCH	Resources are reliable and are accurately recorded.	Resources are reliable but are not accurately recorded.	Some resources may be questionable, but are accurately recorded.	Few resources are reliable, though they may be accurately recorded.	Resources are not recorded.	
COMMENTS:						

ELECTRIFICATION OF THE U.S. PRESENTATION RUBRIC

Performance	Exceeds Expectations (5–6)	Meets Expectations (3–4)	Needs Improvement (1–2)	Score
Information	• Individual or team include many interesting facts and covers all the significant people and/or events.	• Individual or team include some interesting facts and introduces many significant people and/or events.	• Individual or team include a few interesting facts and omits many significant people and/or events.	
Ideas and Organization	• There is a clear organizational strategy. • Presentation includes both an introduction and a conclusion. • Presentation is clear, well organized, and informative. • Team uses presentation time well and presentation is between 5 and 7 minutes long.	• There is an organizational strategy, although it isn't always obvious. • Presentation includes an introduction or a conclusion. • Presentation is semi-organized and informative. • Time is adequately used. Presentation ends on time, but it is either rushed periodically or time is wasted with filler.	• Does not have an organizational strategy. • Presentation does not include an introduction or conclusion. • Presentation is confusing and uninformative. • Manages time poorly. Presentation is too short or too long (less than 5 minutes or longer than 7 minutes).	
Presentation Style	• The presentation is interesting and engaging. Everyone participates. • Presenter(s) is easy to hear and understand. • Presenter(s) uses appropriate language (no slang, poor grammar, infrequent use of filler words such as "uh," "um").	• The presentation is interesting. Most team members participate. • Presenter(s) can be understood, but voice may be too low or unclear. • Presenter(s) uses some inappropriate language (slang, poor grammar, some use of filler words such as "uh," "um").	• The presentation is boring; does not engage the audience. Only one or two team members participate. • Presenter(s) is difficult to understand. • Presenter(s) uses inappropriate language (slang, poor grammar, frequent filler words such as "uh," "um").	
Artifacts and Visual Aids	• Excellent artifacts and/or well-produced visual aids or media are used. • Visual aids/artifacts clarify and enhance the presentation.	• Some visual aids, media, or artifacts are used to present the information. • Visual aids/artifacts are used but do not add to the presentation.	• Does not have any visual aids or media to present the information. • Visual aids are poorly presented or distract from the presentation.	
Response to Audience Questions	• Individual or team responds and seeks clarification of audience questions. • Responses are full of details that clarify. • Understanding of the material is obvious.	• Individual or team responds to audience questions. • Responses are brief and incomplete. • Reflect large gaps in understanding.	• Individual or team fails to respond to questions from audience. • Responses are not accurate or do not reflect understanding of the content.	
Comments:				

4

Lesson Plan 2:
Water Wheels

In this lesson, students explore the concept that energy can be transformed from one form to another. In addition to building devices that transforms energy, students will measure work done in relation to the force expended. Students will gain an understanding of the concept of efficiency, and will be encouraged to optimize their device designs to maximize the amount of work a fixed amount of energy can accomplish. Students will also research renewable and nonrenewable energy sources.

ESSENTIAL QUESTIONS

- What factors need to be considered when measuring work?

- How do we convert units for weight and distance to determine the number of joules being used (unit of measure for work)?

- What does it mean when a person makes the claim that a machine has more output energy than input energy?

- Where did the missing energy go when a machine has more input energy than output energy?

- How can we measure the efficiency of a machine?

- How does having access to a blog, podcast, video, or other virtual platform make collaboration easier? More challenging?

- What is the relationship between the natural resources available in a region to the renewable energy in which a community will invest?

ESTABLISHED GOALS AND OBJECTIVES

At the conclusion of this lesson, students will be able to do the following:

- Explain why the energy output of a machine can never be more than the energy input of the machine

- Distinguish between renewable and nonrenewable energy sources and name several examples of each

- Identify efficiency as the ratio of output energy to input energy

- Compare and contrast the efficiency of devices

- Identify and describe how several sources of renewable energy are used across the U.S.

- Communicate their learning about renewable energy use in the U.S. to an audience using a slideshow

- Identify the basic components of a water wheel

- Utilize the design process (EDP) to build and improve the efficiency of a water wheel

- Explain how friction and heat are related to efficiency

- Use mapping skills to determine where natural resources are being accessed for energy usage

- Determine some of the factors that cause energy sources to be available in a region

- Evaluate renewable energy resources from the perspective of an historical figure and communicate these ideas in writing.

TIME REQUIRED

- 7 days (approximately 45 minutes each day; see Tables 3.6 and 3.7)

MATERIALS

Required Materials for Lesson 2

- STEM Research Notebooks

- Computer with Internet access for viewing videos

- Picture Book: *Energy Island: How one community harnessed the wind and changed their world*, by Allan Drummond [ISBN: 13–978-1250056764]

- Handouts and resources (attached at the end of Lesson 2)

  - Energy Sorting Activity Images

  - Efficiency Activity student handout

  - Renewable Energy Research Project Description student handout

  - Water Wheel Design Challenge student handout

  - Applying the EDP to the Water Wheel Design Challenge

  - Water Wheel Efficiency student handout

- Communicating in Millside Corners student handout

- Regions of the United States student handout

- Rubrics (attached at the end of Lesson 2)

  - Efficiency Activity Rubric

  - Water Wheel Design Challenge Rubric

  - Regional Map Rubric

  - Energy Research Slideshow Rubric

  - Blog, Podcast, or Video Post Rubric

Additional Materials for Efficiency Activity (for each team of 3–4 students)

- 1 pencil

- assortment of 4–6 resistance material samples (see below)

- 2- 1 ¼" fender washers (approx. 8g each)

- 80cm string

- 2 large paper clips

- 60 #8 flat washers

- digital scale (with gram units)

- roll masking tape

- scissors

- calculator

- magnifying lens

Resistance Materials

There should be sufficient material for each student to have 1 sample (about 2cm × 6cm) each of 4–6 materials. Suggested materials include:

- oak tag/note card

- glossy paper

- aluminum foil

- felt

- duct tape

- masking tape

- rough cardboard (paper towel core)

- sand paper

- plastic wrap

- wax paper

- coarse fabric, such as denim

Water Wheel Activity (for each team of 3–4 students)

- 1-gallon waterproof bin or bucket

- 2- 12" plastic rulers (with 3 holes)

- 2- #6 machine screws, 4" long

- 8- #6 flat washers

- 6- #6 hex nuts

- 3/16" dowel rod 10"–12" long

- duct tape or masking tape

- 2 paper clips

- 4' string or twine

- 4 large washers (or similar weight)

- clean 2-liter soda bottle

- scissors

- scale

- meter stick

- Optional materials include: small (6") adjustable wrench and screwdriver

Additional Materials for Energy Research Project (for each team of 3–4 students)

- Internet access for student research

- access to STEM Researchers Google slideshow (www.routledge.com/9781032 618074)

- colored pencils

- ruler

SAFETY NOTES

1. Remind students that personal protective equipment (safety glasses or goggles, aprons, and gloves) must be worn during the setup, hands-on, and takedown segments of activities.

2. Students should use caution when handling scissors and other tools as the sharp points and blades can cut or puncture skin.

3. Tell students to be careful when handling containers. Cut plastic may have sharp edges, which can cut or puncture skin. Plastic can break and cut skin.

4. Immediately wipe up any spilled water to avoid a slip-and-fall hazard.

CONTENT STANDARDS AND KEY VOCABULARY

Table 4.4 lists the content standards from the *NGSS, CCSS,* and the Framework for 21st Century Learning that this lesson addresses, and Table 4.5 presents the key vocabulary. Vocabulary terms are provided for both teacher and student use. Teachers may choose to introduce some or all of the terms to students.

Table 4.4 Content Standards Addressed in STEM Road Map Module Lesson 2

NEXT GENERATION SCIENCE STANDARDS
PERFORMANCE OBJECTIVES
- 4-ESS3-1. Obtain and combine information to describe that energy and fuels are derived from natural resources and their uses affect the environment.
- 4-PS3-2. Make observations to provide evidence that energy can be transferred from place to place by sound, light, heat, and electrical currents.
- 4-PS3–4. Apply scientific ideas to design, test, and refine a device that converts energy from one form to another.

DISCIPLINARY CORE IDEAS
ESS3.A: Natural Resources
- Energy and fuels that humans use are derived from natural sources, and their use affects the environment in multiple ways. Some resources are renewable over time, and others are not.
PS3.A: Definitions of Energy
- Energy can be moved from place to place by mobbing objects or through sound, light, or electric currents.

Table 4.4 (*continued*)

PS3.B: Conservation of Energy and Energy Transfer
- Energy is present whenever there are moving objects, sound, light, or heat. When objects collide, energy can be transferred from one object to another, thereby changing their motion. In such collisions, some energy is typically also transferred to the surrounding air; as a result, the air gets heated and sound is produced.
- Energy can also be transferred from place to place by electric currents, which can then be used locally to produce motion, sound, heat, or light. The currents may have been produced to being with by transforming the energy of motion into electrical energy.

PS3.D: Energy in Chemical Processes and Everyday Life
- The expression "produce energy" typically refers to the conservation of stored energy into a desired form for practical use.

CROSSCUTTING CONCEPTS
Cause and Effect
- Cause and effect relationships are routinely identified and used to explain change.
Energy and Matter
- Energy can be transferred in various ways and between objects.
Systems and System Models
- A system can be described in terms of its components and their interactions.

SCIENCE AND ENGINEERING PRACTICES
Asking Questions and Defining Problems
- Ask questions that can be investigated and predict reasonable outcomes based on patterns such as cause and effect relationships.
Developing and Using Models
- Develop a model to describe phenomena.
- Use a model to test interactions concerning the functioning of a natural system.
Planning and Carrying Out Investigations
- Make observations to produce data to serve as the basis for evidence for an explanation of a phenomenon or test a design solution.
Constructing Explanations and Designing Solutions
- Identify the evidence that supports particular points in an explanation.
- Use evidence (e.g., measurements, observations, patterns) to construct an explanation.
- Generate and compare multiple solutions to a problem based on how well they meet the criteria and constraints of the design solution.
- Apply scientific ideas to solve design problems.
Obtaining, Evaluating, and Communicating Information
- Obtain and combine information from books and other reliable media to explain phenomena.

COMMON CORE STATE STANDARDS FOR MATHEMATICS
MATHEMATICAL PRACTICES
- 4.MP1. Make sense of problems and persevere in solving them.
- 4.MP2. Reason abstractly and quantitatively.
- 4.MP3. Construct viable arguments and critique the reasoning of others.
- 4.MP4. Model with mathematics.

Table 4.4 (*continued*)

- 4.MP5. Use appropriate tools strategically.
- 4.MP6. Attend to precision.

MATHEMATICAL CONTENT

- 4.MD.A.2. Use the four operations to solve word problems involving distances, intervals of time, liquid volumes, masses of objects, and money, including problems involving simple fractions or decimals, and problems that require expressing measurements given in a larger unit in terms of a smaller unit. Represent measurement quantities using diagrams such as number line diagrams that feature a measurement scale.
- 4.MD.B.4. Make a line plot to display a data set of measurements in fractions of a unit (1/2, 1/4, 1/8). Solve problems involving addition and subtraction of fractions by using information presented in line plots.
- 4.MD.C.5. Recognize angles as geometric shapes that are formed wherever two rays share a common endpoint, and understand concepts of angle measurement.

COMMON CORE STATE STANDARDS FOR ENGLISH LANGUAGE ARTS

READING STANDARDS

- RI.4.1. Refer to details and examples in a text when explaining what the text says explicitly and when drawing inferences from the text.
- RI.4.2. Determine the main idea of a text and explain how it is supported by key details, summarize the text.
- RI.4.3. Explain events, procedures, ideas, or concepts in a historical, scientific or technical text, including what happened and why, based on specific information in the text.
- RI.4.4. Determine the meaning of general academic and domain-specific words or phrases in a text relevant to a grade 4 topic or subject area.
- RI.4.6. Compare and contrast a firsthand and secondhand account of the same event or topic; describe the differences in focus and the information provided.
- RI.4.7. Interpret information presented visually, orally, or quantitatively (e.g., in charts, graphs, diagrams, time lines, animations, or interactive elements on Web pages) and explain how the information contributes to an understanding of the text in which it appears.
- RI.4.9. Integrate information from two texts on the same topic in order to write or speak about the subject knowledgeably.

WRITING STANDARDS

- W.4.2. Write informative/explanatory texts to examine a topic and convey ideas and information clearly.
- W.4.6. With some guidance and support from adults, use technology, including the Internet, to produce and publish writing as well as to interact and collaborate with others; demonstrate sufficient command of keyboarding skills to type a minimum of one page in a single sitting.
- W.4.7. Conduct short research projects that build knowledge through investigation of different aspects of a topic.
- W.4.8. Recall relevant information from experiences or gather relevant information from print and digital sources; take notes and categorize information, and provide a list of sources.
- W.4.9. Draw evidence from literary or informational texts to support analysis, reflection, and research.

Table 4.4 (*continued*)

SPEAKING AND LISTENING STANDARDS • SL.4.1. Engage effectively in a range of collaborative discussions (one-on-one, in groups, and teacher-led) with diverse partners on *grade 4 topics and texts*, building on others' ideas and expressing their own clearly. • SL.4.4. Report on a topic or text, tell a story, or recount an experience in an organized manner, using appropriate facts and relevant, descriptive details to support main ideas or themes; speak clearly at an understandable pace. • SL.4.5. Add audio recordings and visual displays to presentations when appropriate to enhance the development of main ideas or themes. *FRAMEWORK FOR 21ST CENTURY LEARNING* • Interdisciplinary Themes (financial, economic, & business literacy; environmental literacy) • Learning and Innovation Skills • Information, Media & Technology Skills • Life and Career Skills

Table 4.5 Key Vocabulary in Lesson 2

Key Vocabulary	Definition
biomass	organic material, such as wood, plant crops, or animal manure
blog	a web log, a public notebook, or journal created for an audience and used to share information online
dam	a barrier constructed to hold back water and raise its level
efficient	performing in the best possible manner with the least waste of effort or time
elevate	raise or lift up to a higher position
force	an energy that causes motion or a change in motion
energy	the ability to work; influenced by motion (kinetic energy), position (potential energy), or the mass of an object ($E=mc^2$)
generator	the motor that produces the electricity in the hydroelectric power system
geothermal	heat energy from the earth's core
hydroelectric power	a renewable energy source for electricity that is generated by the force of moving water
input	in mechanical efficiency, the quantity of energy put into a device

Table 4.5 (*continued*)

Key Vocabulary	Definition
joule	the energy required to exert one newton of force across one meter of distance. For ease of calculations we can approximate a joule as being the force required to lift 100 gm 1 meter
kinetic energy	energy of motion
natural gas	a gas, primarily methane, which comes from the remains of organic materials (plants and animals) that decayed and build up thick layers that were trapped under layers of rock
newton	a measure of force approximately equal to Earth's gravitational pull on an object with mass equal to 102 gm. For ease of calculations we can approximate a newton as 100 gm falling or being lifted
nonrenewable	a material that is only available in limited supplies and can be used up
nuclear power	electricity produced from radioactive materials using nuclear fission
output	in mechanical efficiency, the quantity of energy put out of a device in the form of work
penstock	the pipe system through which water flows toward the turbine in the hydroelectric dam system
petroleum	a fossil fuel that comes from plants and animals that lived long ago
potential energy	energy that is possible due to the position of an object
renewable	a material that is never used up because it replenishes itself
reservoir	a large natural or artificial lake where water is collected and stored for supplying a community, irrigating land, or furnishing power
solar power	electricity produced from the sun's heat and/or light
work	when a force is applied to an object and the object is moved a distance

TEACHER BACKGROUND INFORMATION

In this lesson, students develop a three-dimensional model that will demonstrate how to optimize the efficiency of a dam. To improve the efficiency of a system, students will need to be able to measure that efficiency.

Efficiency

Efficiency is the ratio of useful output energy to input energy, and is expressed as a percent (Eff = [output/input] × 100). Measuring work done is a common method to

determine the amount of energy in a system. Two units are involved in measuring work – the Newton (N) and the joule (J). The newton is a measure of force approximately equal to Earth's gravitational pull on an object with mass equal to 102 gm. For ease of calculations we can approximate one newton as the force required for 102 gm to fall or be lifted. A joule is the energy required to exert one newton of force across one meter of distance. For ease of calculations we can approximate a joule as being the force required to lift 102 gm 1 meter. Conversely, a 102 gm object falling 1 meter has 1 joule of kinetic energy.

No mechanical device is 100% efficient since some output energy is wasted, usually as heat by friction. There will be friction at any place on a mechanical device where two surfaces move against each other, and energy will be lost as heat. Interestingly, the bicycle is generally recognized as the world's most efficient transportation device and one of the most efficient machines ever invented.

Mechanical advantage is often confused with efficiency. Recall that work is force acting across distance. Mechanical advantage refers to adjusting the force required for a certain amount of work by increasing or decreasing the distance over which the force must act. The classic example of mechanical advantage is the lever, a simple machine configured like a teeter-totter with a straight board and a fulcrum. If one moves the fulcrum close to the load end, less force is required on the power end, but the force must be exerted over a much longer distance to move the load a small distance. Conversely, moving the fulcrum close to the power end calls for more force, but the force need not be exerted over a very large distance to move the load a long way.

In contrast, mechanical efficiency is a performance term. Improving efficiency means eliminating waste in the mechanism, usually in the form of friction. In the example below, we discuss mechanical advantage in a multi-speed bicycle. However, no clever combination of gears can compensate for underinflated tires. When a bicycle has underinflated tires, rolling resistance increases dramatically. This wastes energy and reduces cycling efficiency.

The Efficiency Activity in this lesson lets students discover first-hand how various materials differ in the amount of friction they provide. They will discover that, generally, the smoother and harder a substance is, the less friction it offers. It also offers an easy way to visualize the efficiency calculation.

Efficiency and Dams

In a dam, turbines are used to convert the kinetic energy of moving water to mechanical rotation. A turbine's axle is connected to a generator, and when the axle spins, the generator produces AC electrical current. Efficiency gains in this scenario can be found in mechanical upgrades to the turbine and generator equipment.

In this lesson, student teams will build a working water wheel and measure the efficiency by calculating the ratio of work done lifting a weight in relation to the weight of water required for the lift. The big challenge in this activity is to improve the efficiency of their water wheels. This can be done by modifying the turbine blades and reducing friction throughout the apparatus.

In Lesson 1, student teams built a wind turbine which was designed to be powered by the movement of air from the side. In Lesson 2, this device is repurposed as a water-powered device. The main reason for starting with an air-powered version of the turbine is to simplify the classroom lab requirements. Student teams had to solve several problems to build the wind turbine: hub design, blade shape, blade number, etc. A wheel that rotates by air is very similar to one that rotates by water pressure, and students should be able to adapt their wind turbines to a water wheel with minimal modifications.

Renewable vs. Nonrenewable Energy Sources

Much of the world relies on non-renewable energy such as fossil fuels to heat their homes, power electronic devices, and power their cars. Since these resources will not regenerate within a time frame adequate to meet human needs, once these resources are used up, they will be gone forever. Developing technologies that can use renewable resources is therefore critical. Many renewable energy sources are also better for the environment than burning fossil fuels because they produce less pollution which provides for cleaner air and water. Table 4.6 provides a summary of renewable and nonrenewable energy sources.

Table 4.6 Renewable and Nonrenewable Energy Sources

Renewable Energy Sources	Nonrenewable Energy Sources
Water Power – Hydropower is a reliable clean, renewable energy source that converts kinetic energy from falling water into electricity that is used to turn a turbine and create electricity without consuming more water. There are three methods that are used by power plants • Reservoir storage uses a dam to slow the flow of a river and store water in a lake. A portion of the water is released into a river at the base of the dam. This is an effective method for controlling flooding. • Run-of-the-river uses the natural flow of the river to turn the turbines making it a	**Oil (Petroleum)** – Crude oil is a fossil fuel that comes from plants and animals that lived long ago. It pools underground in reservoirs or near the surface in tar sands. Where is it found? It is produced in 31 states and in coastal waters. In 2014 roughly 65% of U.S. produced oil came from Texas, North Dakota, California, and Oklahoma. Petroleum products are: gasoline, diesel fuel, and propane. **Natural Gas** – Natural gas is primarily methane gas. It comes from the remains of

Table 4.6 (*continued*)

Renewable Energy Sources	Nonrenewable Energy Sources
naturalist's choice due to its low impact on the environment. • Pumped storage system uses pumps to keep the water circulating through the system. This is more efficient than the typical reservoir storage since it uses left-over energy at night to pump the water back into the reservoir. Where is it found? The majority of the dams in the U.S. were not built to generate power but rather to provide crop irrigation. The largest number of dams are located in western states. In 2014, Washington state produced 30% of the nation's hydropower. Washington, Idaho, and Oregon use hydroelectricity as their main power source.	organic materials (plants and animals) that decayed and built up thick layers that were trapped under layers of rock. Pressure and heat changed some of the material into tiny bubbles of odorless gas. Where is it found? Some of the natural gas is located inland, but the majority of it is located offshore, deep in the ocean. In 2014, roughly 97% of the gas consumed came from Texas, Pennsylvania, Louisiana, Oklahoma, and Wyoming. Natural gas is a major fuel used to heat buildings and homes. It is also used for cooking, drying clothes, and outdoor lighting.
Solar Power – The primary source of all energy on earth comes from the sun. Solar power is generated directly from the sun to produce thermal (heat) or electric energy. It is converted into electricity in two ways: • Solar cell (photovoltaic cell) panel arrays change sunlight directly into electricity for small and large systems such as solar watches and homes. • Solar power plants concentrate solar energy produce energy to heat a fluid and produce steam to power a generator. Where is it found? Sunshine is solar energy. The amount of sunlight and its intensity varies by location. Deserts contain the most productive solar energy powerhouses. Southern U.S. states produce more than Northern states, Arizona, Hawaii, Nevada, New Mexico, and California are the top producers.	**Coal** – Coal is a combustible black sedimentary rock with large amounts of carbon. It takes millions of years to form which is why it is considered a nonrenewable energy source. Coal is formed primarily in swampy forest areas covered by layers of rock and soil. The heat and pressure turns the plants into one of four types of coal, depending on how much carbon is present. Where is it found? Coal is more widespread than the other nonrenewable resources, but it is primarily found in three regions: the Appalachian coal region, the Interior coal region, and the Western coal region. The greatest number of mines are in Wyoming, West Virginia, Kentucky, Illinois, and Pennsylvania. Many power plants make steam by burning coal. The steam turns turbines which produce electricity. Industries also use coal and coal byproducts.
Wind Power – Wind is considered a renewable energy source because there is always wind on the earth. Energy companies use large	**Uranium (Nuclear Power)** – There is a tremendous amount of energy that bonds the particles of the nucleus of an atom together.

4

Table 4.6 (*continued*)

Renewable Energy Sources	Nonrenewable Energy Sources
windmills called wind turbines due to the turbine generators they use to create electricity. Where is it found? A drawback to wind power is that wind farms need to be placed in an area with an average wind speed of 15 miles per hour. The top wind power producing states are Texas, Iowa, California, Minnesota, and Illinois. Around 3% of U.S. electricity is provided by wind power. This is enough energy to power roughly 10 million homes.	When these bonds are broken, nuclear energy is released. This energy can be used to produce electricity. The way these bonds are broken is through a process called nuclear fission. All nuclear power plants split atoms using this process, and most plants use the uranium atom. Where is it found? Uranium is the fuel used by most nuclear power plants and is considered nonrenewable even though it is a common metal, the uranium that is used (U-235) is rare. Most uranium ore is mined in the western part of the U.S.
Additional Renewable Resources	

Biomass – Biomass is an organic material, such as wood, plant crops, or animal manure. Energy comes from the sun through photosynthesis and is released when biomass is burned or decomposes. Biomass wood and crops can be burned to produce heat, and animal waste is converted into methane gas or ethanol through fermentation.

Biomass fuels are not used often (about 5% of our energy). Of the little that is used, 46% comes from wood and 44% is from converted biofuels.

Where is it found? Anywhere vegetation can grow and animals can graze, biomass can be manufactured. North Dakota, Iowa, Mississippi, Georgia, and North Carolina are the top five U.S. states for producing biomass feedstocks.

Geothermal – This is derived from the earth's core. It can be recovered as steam or as hot water which can be used to heat buildings or generate electricity.

Geothermal reservoirs are deep underground and the heat rises through geysers, hot springs, volcanoes, and fumaroles. The majority of these geothermal hotbeds lie near tectonic plate boundaries, which are marked by the seismic activity and volcanic formations. The most active area is the "Ring of Fire" in the Pacific, which means that California is the #1 producer of geothermal energy, but Nevada, Utah, Hawaii, and Oregon also make use of this renewable energy source.

Geothermal energy uses pipelines to carry hot water and steam to heat buildings, but it also has been used in industry to mine gold and pasteurize milk; however, its most common use is for food dehydration.

Careers in Energy

There is a wide variety of careers associated with energy production. You may wish to introduce some of these careers in this lesson. The following is a list of careers in energy:

- Miners, Gas and Oil Drill Operators, Linemen

- Electric and Power Engineers

- Energy Auditors

- Power Plant Operators

- Safety Managers

- Environmental Engineer

- Future Power Engineer

- Hydrodynamic Engineer

- Chemists who produce hydrogen biologically in landfills and other biomass treatment farms, such as syngas.

- Botanist who can genetically engineer trees and plants to produce more efficient biomass vegetation or energy crops that have greater carbon content and increased oil production.

- Energy Manager, Energy Control Systems Engineer, and Computer modeling, as well as installing and commissioning solar, wind, and micro-renewable technologies

- Wind Farm site prospector, off-shore wind farmer, Environmental Impact Assessor.

Blogging, Podcasting, and Creating Video Clips in the Classroom

Students will have a choice to create blogs, podcasts, or video clips to communicate their learning. All of these artifacts will be similar in content or format to a blog, or a web log, since students who choose to create podcasts or videos will create scripts that are similar to a blog posting. A blog is a bit like an online notebook, except that blogs are typically created for an audience. Blog writing is unlike typical academic writing because it is informal, which tends to be less intimidating to many students. These types of posting opportunities give students a voice to express ideas and learning they are excited about in a safe environment.

These artifacts can be created offline and shared in secure school or class websites. To share these artifacts more widely, the first step is choosing a platform on which to build and publish your artifacts. There are many secure sites where you can do this for free. The top three educational blog sites are:

- https://edublogs.org is a site that lets you create and manage teacher and student sites.

- https://go.fan.school is a platform designed for grades K–12.

- https://wordpress.org is not as simple to use as those specifically designed for educators, but it has some great features. You should note that sites created in this forum will be accessible to the public.

In this module, the emphasis will be on helping students to communicate their ideas. Students will be presented with a fictional scenario in which their historical figures will be competing for the role of moderator at a debate. Encourage students to vary their posts by incorporating images, quotes, and other resources.

COMMON MISCONCEPTIONS

Students will have various types of prior knowledge about the concepts introduced in this lesson. Table 4.7 outlines some common misconceptions students may have concerning these concepts. Because of the breadth of students' experiences, it is not possible to anticipate every misconception that students may bring as they approach this lesson. Incorrect or inaccurate prior understanding of concepts can influence student learning in the future, however, so it is important to be alert to misconceptions such as those presented in the table.

Table 4.7 Common Misconceptions about the Concepts in Lesson 2

Topic	Student Misconception	Explanation
Energy	Energy is found only in living things.	Energy is the ability to produce a change; there are many forms of energy, such as heat, light, and sound. Living things are able to convert energy into other types of energy (e.g., converting food into energy for muscles).
	Energy is a fuel, like gasoline.	Fuel is a source of energy and is burned to create power or heat.
	Work and labor are the same thing.	Work, in scientific terms, does not relate to our perception of an activity, so the amount of work done, in scientific terms, an hour running and playing outside may be greater than the amount of work done staying inside and studying for an hour.
	Renewable energy sources are too expensive for widespread use.	As technologies improve, the cost of producing renewable energy is decreasing and in many areas around the world the cost of renewable energy such as hydropower, wind, and solar is quite similar to that of fossil fuels.

PREPARATION FOR LESSON 2

Review the teacher background information provided, assemble materials for lesson, duplicate student handouts, and preview the slideshow included within the Learning Plan Components.

Prior to class gather an assortment of resistance materials for the Efficiency Activity. The wider the variety of material, the better. There should be sufficient material for each team to have a few small samples (2cm × 6cm) of each material. Suggested materials include oak tag/note card, glossy paper, aluminum foil, felt, duct tape, masking tape, rough cardboard (such as a paper towel core), sand paper, plastic wrap, wax paper, and coarse fabric such as denim. Create space in the classroom to accommodate one station for each team and provide each station with a different type of resistance material. Teams will construct pulleys at their station using one type of resistance material and then will rotate through the stations making observations of the efficiency characteristics of the resistance material featured at that station. Be sure that there are samples of each material, sized to fit the data sheet, for each student in the class at all stations. Count out 60 of the #8 flat washers for each station and place them in bags at each station.

Be prepared to project an image of a constructed water wheel for the Water Wheel Design Challenge, or build an example to show students. Instructions for building a water wheel are included on the Water Wheel Design Challenge student handout. You may wish to enlist the assistance of adult volunteers to work with teams as students create their water wheels.

Students will create periodic posts about their learning in this module. You may wish to provide students a choice of format for their posts, such as blog, podcast, or videoclip. You should also decide how frequently students will create posts (for example, once a week or twice a week) and whether and how these posts will be shared with the school community and with the larger community online. Create a safe, secure, kid-friendly blog platform for your students and/or secure permission for students' artifacts to be posted on a class or school website. Before beginning this assignment, check with your school administrator for a written guideline for student blogging and use this to develop your goals and expectations. For example, some schools may not allow photos of students on public posts or may require written permission from a parent to participate in an assignment to be posted to a website.

Secure two or three days each week in the computer or technology lab for student research and blogging, podcasting, and vide creation if necessary.

Visit your local library to compile a collection of fiction books about the wind or wind mills that can be used to compare and contrast kinetic and potential energy, and nonfiction books about natural resources and biographies of some of the men and women who were chosen for the character study project. The librarian may put a collection together for you if you call ahead.

LEARNING PLAN COMPONENTS
Introductory Activity/Engagement

Connection to the Challenge: Begin each day of this lesson by directing students' attention to the module challenge, Big Changes for Millside Corners Design Challenge. Hold a brief class discussion each day of how students' learning in the previous days' lessons contributed to their ability to complete the challenge. You may wish to create a class list of key ideas on chart paper.

Science Class and ELA and Social Studies Connections: Ask students the following question to introduce the idea of natural resources being used for energy:

What are some examples of ways that natural resources are transformed into energy? [Don't let students miss the obvious; for example, plants store energy in the form of sugars and starches, animals and people eat plants and the stored energy provides life.]

Tell students that you are going to read a book together in which they will learn about a community has many excuses for not using natural resources for heat, light, and transportation. Ask students what some reasons may be that people choose not to use natural resources as energy sources? Have students respond to the following question in their STEM Research Notebooks:

If you lived on an island or an area where electrical power is limited, what could you and your family do to use less electricity?

Read aloud the book *Energy Island* by Allan Drummond. This is a first person account of how a community of regular people can make an impact by changing the way they do everyday life. The message is that it takes a willful decision to become energy independent. This book also offers a first-person voice to compare to the third-person accounts students read as they collect biographical information in their character studies. The book also offers students practical ideas of ways to save energy. After reading the book, hold a class discussion, asking questions such as:

- What are some of the conditions that made Samso a good location for an energy independence plan?

- Compare and contrast how energy was used before and after they decided to embrace this idea.

- What were some of the obstacles the teacher (Mr. Hermansen) had to overcome?

- How practical were the students' ideas for becoming energy independent?

- Why didn't the people on the island embrace this right away? What was the disaster that changed their minds?

- How can we begin making changes in our lifestyle to become more energy efficient?

Next, students will participate in an activity in which they distinguish renewable from nonrenewable energy sources.

ENERGY SORTING ACTIVITY

Introduce energy resources to students by exploring as a class a resource such as the US Energy Information Administration's Energy Kids website (*https://www.eia.gov/kids/*).

Next, engage students in an Energy Sorting Activity to ensure they know the difference between renewable and nonrenewable energy. Hand out one set of the Energy Sorting Activity images to each team, have students cut apart the images and then work together to sort the images into renewable and non-renewable categories. After teams have completed sorting their images, review the images as a class and discuss how teams classified each image.

Mathematics Connection: Not applicable

Activity/Exploration

Science Class and Mathematics Connection: Students will explore the concept of efficiency in the Efficiency Activity.

Efficiency Activity

This activity is a simple introduction to the concept of efficiency, an essential consideration in the water wheel activity that comes later in this lesson. Efficiency is the ratio of output energy to input energy, and is expressed as a percent (efficiency = [output/input] × 100).

Hold a class discussion about energy inputs and outputs in a machine such as a bicycle, asking questions such as:

- What is the input into this machine that makes it work?

- What is the output?

- Compare and contrast input and output in regards to energy.

- What does it mean to be efficient? How does efficiency relate to input and output of energy?

- Why do you suppose people say the bicycle is one of the most efficient machines ever invented?

- As you consider the bicycle, what might be ways that an engineer could improve the efficiency of this machine?

To explore efficiency, student teams will construct a primitive pulley to lift a weight. Instructions are provided on the Efficiency Activity student handout. The pulley consists of a string with a hook at each end. The string is suspended at its center point over a pencil taped to a desk. Students start out with a single 2″ fender washer on each hook, so the two hooks are balanced and hanging the same distance below the pencil. Students add weight to one hook (the power hook) until the total mass of the hook is sufficient to lift the weight on the other hook (the load hook).

The ratio of the total mass on the load hook divided by the total mass on the power hook gives the efficiency of the device (eff = [output/input] × 100). Students will perform several trials using pencils modified by various resistance materials (e.g., sandpaper, plastic, felt, aluminum foil, etc.) as they rotate through stations. The different materials vary the amount of resistance encountered by the string as it moves across the pencil. The more resistance the string encounters, the less efficient the device will be.

Introduce the concept of efficiency with an explanation of the terms "input" and "output" as they relate to energy. A 100% efficient device will produce exactly as much work as the energy that is put into it. If a machine is 100% efficient, it will run forever on the initial energy it starts with. This is the idea behind the notion of a perpetual motion machine; creating such a machine is a goal that has been popular with tinkerers and engineers since the Middle Ages.

Distribute the Efficiency Activity student handouts to each student. Have each team go to one station. Have students examine the resistance materials and predict the resistance that each will provide by ranking the materials 1 (least resistance) to 6 (most resistant) and recording their predictions on the Resistance Material Data sheet on the Efficiency Activity Student handout. Next, have each team prepare their station by following the instructions provided on the Efficiency Activity student handout.

After teams have prepared their pulleys, have them follow the procedure on the Efficiency Activity student handout to make observations and record their findings on the Efficiency Data Table. Next, teams should rotate through each station with their string, weights, and data sheet, testing the resistance material at each station and recording findings on the Efficiency Data Table.

After teams have rotated through all stations and completed their Efficiency Data Tables, have them revisit the Resistance Material Data table, recording the actual rankings of the materials and comparing these to their predictions.

Paula Schoeff et al.

ELA Connection: Students will create blogs, podcasts, or video clips throughout the module and their work on the Big Changes for Millside Corners Design Challenge. Suggested topics are included on the Communicating in Millside Corners student handout.

Communicating in Millside Corners

Hand out the Communicating in Millside Corners student handout to each student. Tell students that Professor Ipswitch has decided to hold a debate that will take place during the Fossil Fair that will be held in Millside Corners. He expects the debate to be heated, so he is looking for an impartial moderator who is willing to tackle this responsibility. He or she needs to be well informed, so the Professor is using blog, podcast, and video posts to help him make his selection. Tell students that they will create two posts each week (or the frequency and number of posts you decided on – see Preparation for Lesson 1, p. XX). Professor Ipswitch will use these posts to help him select a well-prepared moderator. Tell students that they should assume the role of their character as they address the topics.

Hold a class discussion about blogging, podcasting, and creating videos, asking students to respond to questions such as:

- How are blogs, podcasts, and video posts similar to face-to-face conversations? How are these forms of communication different from conversations with your peers?

- People who create blogs, podcasts, or video posts often express their opinions about topics openly and other people will post comments. Some responders will agree with the author and others will disagree. When posting, what is the appropriate way to respond if someone disagrees with your views?

- Suppose someone has posted an opinion that is offensive to you or is an idea that you know is false. What would be the best way to respond to this author?

Hand out the Blog, Podcast, and Video Post Rubric and review the criteria with students. Have students each create their first posting.

Social Studies Connection: Students will investigate renewable energy in the Renewable Energy Research and Mapping Activity.

Renewable Energy Research and Mapping Activity

Remind students that in the *Energy Island* story, Energy Island is a small island between two peninsulas of Denmark, and that it is very windy and there is a lot of water. Ask students if they think it is a reasonable expectation of Soren Hermansen to completely stop using all nonrenewable resources of energy and to explain their reasons for their responses.

Have students work together in teams to consider the following statement: *Some people argue that converting to renewable energy sources has negative effects on nature, the climate, and food production that outweigh its benefits.* Have teams discuss whether they agree or disagree with this statement and whether they believe that renewable energy resources should be used if there are negative consequences.

After teams have discussed the issue, take a class poll to learn how many students agree and how many disagree. Next, take a class poll of how many students believe that renewable energy sources can supply all of society's electricity needs and how many do not believe this is possible.

Tell students that their task in this activity is to research how renewable resources have been used to produce energy in the United States.

Distribute the Regions of the United States student handout to each student. As a class, discuss where each of the five regions listed below are, and have students shade each region with a different colored pencil and create a map key for the regions.

- Region 1: Northeast Region

- Region 2: Southeast Region

- Region 3: Midwest Region

- Region 4: Southwest Region

- Region 5: West Region

Next, assign one region to each team. Tell students that each team will create a slideshow presentation to explain how renewable energy resources have been used to produce energy in their assigned region. Provide students with the STEM Researchers template that has been provided at www.routledge.com/9781032618074. Hand out the Renewable Energy Research Project Description student handout and the Renewable Energy Presentation rubric to each student and review with the class. Each student should create a map of their region and pinpoint the renewable resources that are in that region. Distribute the Regional Map rubric and review the rubric with students.

Explanation

Science class: Have students complete a STEM Research Notebook entry about the Efficiency Activity with the following information responding to the following prompts:

- Describe an ideal material to use between two surfaces to reduce friction.

- In our activity, friction reduced efficiency. Describe a situation or device where the goal is increased friction (bike brakes, rubber feet on a ladder, sand paper, gym shoes, etc.).

- Does friction resistance exist between non-solid objects like air or water?

- Explain the following phrase in relation to the pulleys they constructed: "Work happens when a force overcomes resistance and moves something."

Mathematics Connection: Show students the sample water wheel you created and tell them that they will create water wheels later in the lesson and work to improve the wheels' efficiency. First, however, they need to be able to measure efficiency, which means that they need to know how to measure how much work the water wheel does. The following is an optional mathematics activity that should be undertaken as a whole class since the mathematics content is above a fourth grade level.

Introduce the concept that the amount of work a machine does can be expressed in units of joules, and that one joule is defined as lifting something that weighs 102 grams 1 meter into the air, against the pull of gravity.

The water wheel will lift a small weight from the floor to the level of the axle by winding the string as the wheel turns under the force of falling water as it is being poured from a half gallon or 2-liter bottle onto the turbine. Student teams will calculate the amount of work done in joules as the water wheel raises the weight.

As a class, work to arrive at a reasonably repeatable value for the amount of work the water wheel can do with the water in a single 2-liter bottle (this will be a series of trials where the team determines the optimal amount of weight to lift so they get a good measurement for the distance raised). The goal is to be able to maintain the spinning water wheel throughout the whole movement. If the weight is too heavy, the wheel will stall because the downward force of the water is not sufficient to lift the weight. If the wheel has poor design, it will stall because it cannot maintain rotation in the water stream. This often happens when the wheel has too few blades.

For example, if the wheel raises 45 grams a distance of 30 inches, you would calculate work in joules with the following calculations:

- 1 in. = 2.54 cm (100 cm = 1 meter)

- 30 in. × 2.54 cm/in. = 76.2 cm or 0.762 meters

- $45/102 \times 0.76 = 0.34$ joules

Once you can get repeated successful lifts, you will need to calculate the energy going into the water wheel. The falling water is delivering a certain amount of energy, also measured in joules. The calculation for the energy of a falling body is the similar to the one for a lifted body: one joule is approximately equal to 1 newton (102 grams) falling 1 meter of distance with the pull of gravity.

Measure the amount of water needed to raise the weight using the following calculations:

- Mass of water (in grams) divided by 102 (since joules are calculated in newtons, e.g., 102 gm)

- Multiply the answer by the distance the water falls in meters.

For example: 1,500 gm water dropped 0.10 m (approx. 4 inches)

- The mas of the water weighed 15 gm, this is multiplied by 100 to get 1,500 gm (Helpful Hint: water weighs 1 gm per ml. Liquid volume of water in ml converts to the same number in gm.)

- 1 in. = 2.54 cm (100 centimeters = 1 meter)

- 4 in × 2.54 cm/in = 10.16 cm or 0.10 meters

- 1500/102 × 0.10 = 1.47 joules

If we know the amount of energy going into the device and the amount of energy coming out of the device, we can calculate efficiency. Efficiency is measured as a percentage. It is the ratio of work out (output) divided by work in (input) or (output/input) × 100 = efficiency.

Using the examples above, we did .34 joules worth of work (output) with 1.47 joules of falling water energy (input).

Example: 0.34 joules/1.47 joules × 100 = 23.13% efficiency.

Social Studies Connection: Have each team share its Renewable Energy Research presentation with the class. Create a class chart listing each of the regions of the U.S., the types of renewable energy resources used there, and the reasons why those resources are used in that region (e.g., availability of resource, landforms and geography).

ELA Connection: In fourth grade, students are exploring nonfiction books and finding information from magazines, picture books, technical trade books, and a variety of research resources. Students encountered a non-fiction, first-person account of the transformation of a Dutch island community into an energy independent area when they read Energy Island. Ask students for their ideas about how the writing was different in this book than it is in their science textbooks. Introduce the idea to students that in each piece of writing, the author adopts a particular perspective or voice. Ask students to identify who the narrator is in the book Energy Island versus who the narrator is in their textbooks. Introduce the concept of first person versus third person voice using the information in the chart below.

First Person	Third Person
Written by a person who is experiencing the event	Written by a person who has read about or interviewed a person who has an experience
Describes the person's thoughts and feelings	Narrator tells about the people's thoughts and feelings as an observation
My story	Another person's story
Keywords: I, me, my – we, us	Uses pronouns: he, she, him, her – they, them, their
Examples of 1st person accounts: *Diary of a Wimpy Kid* by Jeff Kinney [ISBN-13: 978–0810993136] *All the Places to Love* by Patricia MacLachlan [ISBN-13: 978–0060210984] *Green Eggs and Ham* by Dr. Seuss [ISBN-13: 978–0394800165]	Example of 3rd person accounts: *Always Room for One More* by Sorche Nic Leodhas [ISBN-13: 978–0805003307] *Frog and Toad Are Friends* by Arthur Lobel [ISBN-13: 978–0064440202] *Sir Princess Petra Adventures* by Diane Mae Robinson [ISBN-13: 978–1613462645]

Elaboration/Application of Knowledge

Science Class and Mathematics Connection: Students will apply their learning about efficiency as they create water wheels and work to improve their efficiency in the Water Wheel Design Challenge.

Water Wheel Design Challenge

This activity offers students an opportunity to explore the concept that energy can be transformed from one form to another by creating a simple turbine. In addition to building a device that transforms energy, an option is to have students measure work done in relation to the force expended (i.e., calculate efficiency). Students will be encouraged to optimize their designs to maximize the amount of work a fixed amount of energy can accomplish.

Student teams will build water wheel devices that utilize the wheel's mechanical movement to lift a weight on a string. They will follow instructions for constructing the water wheel, but once they have a working water wheel, teams will focus on improving the wheel's efficiency.

Introduce the activity by holding a class discussion about using water to do work by asking questions such as:

- Have you ever seen a machine that was powered by water? How did it work? *Some students may have seen a hydropower generator, but a much more common water-powered machine is an oscillating or spinning lawn sprinkler.*

- In Lesson 1, you built a wind turbine that was powered by air coming in from one side. Could the wind turbine be converted to spin when water is used instead?

- How might a water-powered turbine be the same or different from a wind-powered turbine?

- Which has more force moving air or moving water? Explain your reasoning.

Each student team should have a waterproof version of the wind turbine from Lesson 1. This turbine will be repurposed as the power plant of the water wheel. Distribute a copy of the Water Wheel Design Challenge student handout to each student and a copy of the EDP Applied to the Water Wheel Design Challenge handout to each team.

Review the handouts with students. First, student teams should follow the instructions in the Water Wheel Design Challenge student handout to build a frame to hold the turbine. The frame consists of two 12″ plastic rulers. One ruler, the stationary frame, is secured to the inside of the plastic tub with duct tape. The machine screws serve as the top and bottom braces of the frame and hold the second ruler out from the first. The turbine rotates on the horizontal axle between the two rulers.

After student teams have created their water wheels and calculated their efficiency, they are challenged to improve the efficiency of their water wheels. Remind students that energy cannot be created or destroyed so this means that energy is being lost in their water wheels. The key to improving efficiency is looking for wasted energy. Ask students to share their ideas about where energy may be wasted. Create a class list of students' ideas. Tell students that energy is wasted in the water wheels in three main ways:

1. Water wasted by missing the blades – observe the water as it falls against the blades. To investigate this, ask the following questions:

   - How many blades are in contact with moving water at any given time?

   - Is the water stream so big that some water is missing the blades altogether?

2. Too much friction on the axle. To investigate this, ask the following questions:

   - Is the axle binding in the frames (twisted or rubbing)?

   - Are the spacers that keep the axle in place rubbing against the frames?

3. Trying to lift too much weight. To investigate this, ask the following questions:

- Does the wheel spin slowly?

- If the wheel could spin faster with less load, would it be more efficient?

Distribute the Water Wheel Efficiency student handouts to each student. Teams should consider each of the above questions and devise ways to improve the efficiency of their water wheels. You have the option of having students perform efficiency calculations similar to those you demonstrated (see Explanation section, p. XX). Remind students that the aim is to find wasted energy and improve the device.

ELA Connection: Have half the class write a description of their day from the time they get up until the time they arrive at school from a first-person perspective. Have the other half of the class write the same description about their day, but from a third person perspective. These descriptions should be about 6–7 sentences in length. After students have written their descriptions, pair students who wrote from the first and third person perspectives. Have students exchange their descriptions and read their partners' description and then hold a discussion about how the two descriptions were different and the same in terms of the voice used. Have student pairs share their ideas with the class.

Social Studies Connection: As a class, discuss the ways renewable energy is used in your local community. Ask students to name ways that they have seen renewable energy used locally, creating a class list. Challenge students to go on a renewable energy scavenger hunt in the classroom, looking for evidence of how renewable energy is being used (e.g., solar powered calculators, passive solar heat through windows). Create a class list of students' responses. Next, challenge students to extend the scavenger hunt to their out of school experiences, and ask students to bring in examples of devices powered by renewable energy sources they see outside of school (e.g., solar powered signs, wind turbines, wind chimes). Have students make a list of the items and share them in class.

An option for this lesson is to have students read blogs and articles about renewable energy sources. Have each team read a different article and then summarize the article for the class. Examples of articles include the following:

- Google Green Blog: "Understanding Our Goal: What It Means to Be Powered by 100% Renewable Energy" – www.googlegreenblog.blogspot.com/2016/02/google-green-blog-what-it-means-to-be_8.html

- Inter Press Service: "Innovative Project to Provide Renewable Energy 24/7 to Chilean Village" – www.ipsnews.net/2016/01/innovative-project-to-provide-renewable-energy-247-in-chilean-village/

Evaluation/Assessment

Students may be assessed on the following performance tasks and other measures listed.

Performance Tasks

- Energy Sorting Activity
- Efficiency Activity
- Water Wheel Design Challenge
- Energy Research slideshow
- Renewable Energy Research
- Blog, podcast, or video posts

Other Measures

- Teacher observations
- STEM Research Notebook entries
- Student participation in teams

INTERNET RESOURCES

Blogging resources

- https://edublogs.org
- https://go.fan.school
- https://wordpress.org

Energy resources information

- https://www.eia.gov/kids/

Renewable Energy STEM Researchers slideshow template

- www.routledge.com/9781032618074

Renewable energy blogs and articles

- www.googlegreenblog.blogspot.com/2016/02/google-green-blog-what-it-means-to-be_8.html
- www.ipsnews.net/2016/01/innovative-project-to-provide-renewable-energy-247-in-chilean-village/

ENERGY SORTING ACTIVITY IMAGES

Figure 4.4 Electric generating plant

Figure 4.5 Hoover hydroelectric power dam

Figure 4.6 Candle

Figure 4.7 Steam engine

ENERGY SORTING ACTIVITY IMAGES

Figure 4.8 Vehicle

Figure 4.9 Electric car

Figure 4.1 Wind Turbine

Figure 4.10 Wood fire

4 Paula Schoeff et al.

ENERGY SORTING ACTIVITY IMAGES

Figure 4.11 Nuclear power plant

Figure 4.12 Tidal power

Figure 4.13 Battery powered device

Figure 4.14 Hot springs – geothermal plant

Figure 4.15 Solar array

Figure 4.16 Gas stove

ENERGY SORTING ACTIVITY IMAGES

Figure 4.17 Bike rider

Figure 4.18 Lightning

Figure 4.19 Battery

Figure 4.20 Corn

Paula Schoeff et al.

EFFICIENCY ACTIVITY

NAME:_____   TEAM NAME:_____

Procedure:

Prepare Pulleys: Wrap the resistance material around the pencil just behind the metal eraser ferrule. Secure the material with masking tape at each end. [Note: lay the material longwise along the pencil instead of winding it around in several layers.] Tape the pencil to the table so that the portion covered by the resistance material hangs over the floor.

Assemble String and Hooks: Measure and cut a piece of string 80cm (about 30") long. Unfold paper clips to make two large hooks and tie one to each end. Mark the center point of the string with a pen or marker. Put one fender washer on each hook. Identify the power hook with a distinctive shape or mark.

Examine a sample of each resistance material and make predictions about which material will make the most efficient pulley and which will make the least efficient. Arrange the samples on the data collection sheet in order from the predicted most efficient (1) to the predicted least efficient (6). Tape the samples in place on the data sheet and add notes explaining the reasons for the predictions.

EFFICIENCY ACTIVITY

Resistance Material Table

Predicted Rank	Final Rank	Material Sample	Predictions	Observations
1				
2				
3				
4				
5				
6				

Beginning with your home station, you will rotate through each station. At each station, test to determine how much force is required on the power hook to move the load hook by doing the following:

- Center the string on the pulley's resistance material with the hooks hanging down, loaded with one 1 1/4" fender washer on each side. Make sure the hooks aren't tangled or hanging on each other.

- Add small washers, one at a time, to the power hook.

- When the power hook has enough small washers added that it lifts the load hook, stop adding small washers (potential energy has become kinetic energy).

- Record the input and output on the Efficiency Data Table.

Paula Schoeff et al.

EFFICIENCY ACTIVITY

To find the hook masses do the following:

- Zero the scale and weigh the power hook, with the fender washer and all of the small washers needed to make the load move on it.

- Zero the scale and weigh the load hook with its fender washer on it.

- Record the masses in the data sheet on the row that matches the material.

Efficiency Data Table					
Material	Load Hook Mass (output)	Power Hook Mass (input)	Formula eff = (output/input) × 100	Efficiency	Final Rank (1 is most efficient)

RENEWABLE ENERGY RESEARCH PROJECT DESCRIPTION

Each team will research a different region of the United States. Each team member will be responsible for asking questions, researching, and contributing answers.

- Write your notes in your STEM research notebook as an outline.

- After you have your information, create a slideshow to share with the class.

As you prepare your slideshow include the following:

_____ The states in your assigned region

_____ The climate (identifying the biome(s) may be helpful)

_____ The major bodies of water and landforms

_____ The natural resources that are located in your region

_____ Answers to the following questions

How does this region use their resources to produce energy?

★ Are there hydroelectric power plants and dams on its rivers and lakes?

★ Are there geothermal electric plants near its Hot Springs?

★ Are biomass sources (soybeans and manure) used as energy sources?

★ Is wind being captured with windmills to generate power?

★ Are ocean's tides being used to create power?

★ Is electricity being generated with solar cell panels or other solar technologies?

In your research you will find great images and possibly videos or slideshows. **Be Creative!** Any media that will help your team make connections between the features and characteristics of your region and the region's available natural resources will be helpful as we prepare for the debate and seek to make decisions about using the resources in our own community more effectively.

RENEWABLE ENERGY RESEARCH PROJECT DESCRIPTION

Links that you might find helpful:

- Energy.gov Electric Power/Energy Sources/Energy Efficiency: http://www.energy.gov/science-innovation/

- Duckster: http://www.ducksters.com/science/environment/wind_power.php

- http://www.nrdc.org/energy/renewables/

- http://photos1.blogger.com/blogger/697/383/1600/2006%20map.gif

While you are working on your research, create a second visual for your presentation. This map will be used to show the class where the resources are in your region – and where the resources are being used as renewable energy.

- Create a good title for your map that will describe how it is being used.

- Draw a map of the REGION showing major landforms (mountains, rivers, big lakes, etc.).

- Create a map key for the natural resources that are located in this region.

- Choose your colors and consider how you want to label your map so its appearance is improved.

- The following should be included in your map:

  _____ the name of your region in its title

  _____ all the states in your region labeled correctly

  _____ each state represented with a different color

  _____ the oceans, major lakes, and rivers are labeled

  _____ the major mountain ranges are represented and labeled

  _____ a compass rose

  _____ a key/legend is used to explain the symbols used on the map

WATER WHEEL DESIGN CHALLENGE

Name _____   **Date** _____

In this activity, you will build a water wheel that can transform the force of falling water into mechanical movement that lifts a weight. The device you build will be used for several activities so take your time and follow the instructions carefully.

Water Wheel – Basic Steps
1. Gather materials
2. Build stationary frame
3. Mount wheel to axle
4. Add removable frame section
5. Balance and center wheel in frame
6. Measure work weight and lift string
7. Attach weight and string to axle
8. Position assembly so weight hangs freely just above the floor

1. Gather Materials	• STEM Research Notebook • 1-gallon waterproof tub or bucket • 2- 12" plastic rulers (w/ 3 holes) • 2- #6 x 3" machine screws • 8- #6 flat washers • 6- #6 hex nuts • 3/16 dowel rod 10–12" long • duct tape • Wind turbine from Lesson 1 • 4' string or twine • 4- 2" washers (or similar weight) • clean 2-liter soda bottle • scissors • scale • meter stick • Applying the EDP to the Water Wheel Design Challenge handout

Paula Schoeff et al.

WATER WHEEL DESIGN CHALLENGE

2. Build Stationary Frame
 	
  1. Put a washer on each of the two #6 machine screws.
 	
  2. Pass each screw through the slotted holes furthest from the center of the ruler.
 	
  3. Add a washer on each screw.
 	
  4. Thread a #6 nut onto each screw.
 	
  5. Tighten both nuts so the screws are snug in the ruler.
	Build Stationary Frame (part 2)
	
	  1. The ruler should be fastened to one side of the plastic tub with duct tape.
	
	  2. There are two important requirements for this step:
	    • The ruler should be high enough that you can see through the center hole over the top of the side.
	    • The ruler should be straight up and down.
	
	  3. Fasten the bottom of the ruler to the tub with duct tape.
	
	  4. Add a second piece of duct tape near the top of the side of the tub.
	
	  5. You may need to make a spacer from a folded card to hold the ruler straight up and down.
	
	  6. Fasten the ruler near the top of the tub with the second piece of duct tape.

3. Mount Wheel to Axle
 	
  1. Modify the wind turbine from Lesson 1 to fit in the Water Turbine frame.
 	
  2. Fasten the wheel to the axle (stick) so that when the wheel turns, the axle turns.
 	
  3. Wrap tape around the end of the straw so straw is stuck to axle.
 	
  4. Wheel should be close to one end of the stick.
	4. Add Removable Frame Section
	
	  1. Thread one #6 nut on to each screw on the frame built in step 3.
	    • Thread each nut on so it is 1 inch from the end of the screw.
	    • Add one #6 washer on to each screw.
	
	  2. Pass the long end of the axle through the center hole of the ruler mounted in the tub.
	
	  3. Add the second ruler by passing the short end of the axle through the center hole of the second ruler.
	
	  4. Secure the second ruler to the bottom of the tub using duct tape.

WATER WHEEL DESIGN CHALLENGE

4. Add Removable Frame (part 2)	1. Mount the second ruler on the two #6 screws. 2. Add one #6 washer to each screw. 3. Thread one #6 nut on to each screw. 4. Tighten the nuts so the second ruler is secure. 5. Use duct tape to fasten the second ruler to the bottom of the tub.
5. Balance and Center Wheel in Frame	1. Center the water wheel in the frame so it rotates without hitting or rubbing the frame on either side. 2. Build up the axle outside each side of the frame to keep the wheel from moving side to side. • Wrap tape around the axle **OR** • Slide small pieces of straw on the axle on each side of the frame and tape in place. 3. The wheel should spin freely in the frame. 4. The axle should turn as the wheel turns.
6. Measure Work Weight and Lift String	1. Tie one end of the string around the washers (or weights). 2. Weigh the mass of weights and string and record the mass in your STEM research notebook to use later.

STUDENT HANDOUT, PAGE 4 OF 4

WATER WHEEL DESIGN CHALLENGE

7. Attach Weight and String to Axle	1. Cut out two circles of oak tag and punch holes in the middle of each.
	2. Slide the circles on the long end of the axle.
	3. Wrap tape around the end of the axle to keep the circles from sliding off.
	4. Wrap tape between the circles to keep them 2" – 3" apart. This should keep one circle in place near the end of the axle.
	5. Wrap tape on the axle to keep the second circle in place.
	6. Tie the free end of string tightly to the axle between the two circles.
	7. Make sure the weights are hanging freely over the edge of the desk.
	8. Measure the length of the string and write this length in your STEM research notebook to use later.
8. Test Water Wheel	1. Pour water over the blades of the water wheel on one side.
	2. The wheel should turn and lift the weight off the ground by winding the string.
	3. Adjust the wheel so it turns freely and lifts the weights.
	4. If the wheel cannot lift the weights, change the side of the wheel where you pour the water.
	5. If the wheel still cannot lift the weights, remove some of the weight and record the new weight in your STEM research notebook.

Figure 4.21

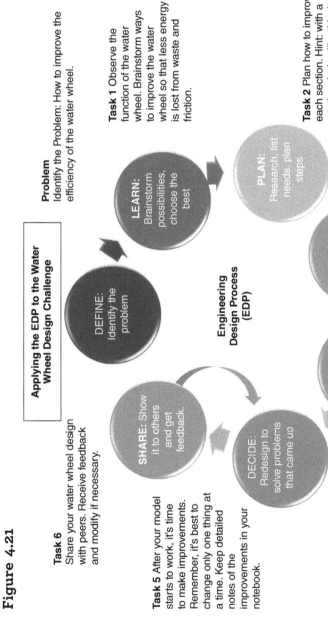

Applying the EDP to the Water Wheel Design Challenge

Engineering Design Process (EDP)

Problem
Identify the Problem: How to improve the efficiency of the water wheel.

Task 1 Observe the function of the water wheel. Brainstorm ways to improve the water wheel so that less energy is lost from waste and friction.

Task 2 Plan how to improve each section. Hint: with a rotating device like this, it is best to solve the problems from the center (axle) out...axle... hub... blades

Make sketches of your plans in your notebook.

Task 3 Get to work! Modify your model using the plan you made. Hint: the three main areas of improvement are wasted water, axle friction, and wheel spin.

Task 4 Test your model. Calculate the work output in joules and the water energy input in joules. Output/input is efficiency.

Task 5 After your model starts to work, it's time to make improvements. Remember, it's best to change only one thing at a time. Keep detailed notes of the improvements in your notebook.

Task 6
Share your water wheel design with peers. Receive feedback and modify if necessary.

LEARN: Brainstorm possibilities, choose the best

PLAN: Research, list needs, plan steps

DEFINE: Identify the problem

TRY: Follow your plan and build a model

SHARE: Show it to others and get feedback

DECIDE: Redesign to solve problems that came up

TEST: Try it out. What works? What doesn't?

4

Paula Schoeff et al.

WATER WHEEL EFFICIENCY

Name _____ **Date** _____

Use this worksheet to calculate your water wheel efficiency.

Efficiency measures how well a machine does a certain kind of work. Efficiency is a ratio or comparison. To calculate an efficiency ratio, we need to know two things:

- **OUTPUT:** How much useful work is done?

- **INPUT:** How much force is needed to do the work?

The formula for efficiency is: OUTPUT/INPUT x 100

The work of the water wheel is to lift a washer from the floor when the axle winds up the string. The energy is supplied by a stream of water pushing against the blades of the water wheel. To calculate the water wheel efficiency, **divide the work done when the washer is raised by the force of the falling water.**

Sketch the Water Wheel showing the washer being lifted and water falling. Label the direction of the forces.

Work is done when force overcomes resistance and moves something.

Both the water falling and the washers being lifted are examples of work.

- For the washers being lifted, force acts against gravity's pull.

- For water falling, the water exerts force because it is falling with gravity's pull.

Calculate the force in newtons (N) by dividing the mass of the washer by 102.

WATER WHEEL EFFICIENCY

**Important! Weigh only the water used – that which fell into the bin. Any water remaining in the bottle was unused and should not be included in the water mass.

Step 1: Force	Mass Being Moved	÷	Newton Conversion	=	Force in Newtons
OUTPUT	Mass of washers _____ grams	÷	102	=	Force to lift washers _____ newtons
INPUT	Mass of water used _____grams	÷	102	=	Force of falling water _____ newtons
Step 2: Distance	**Mass Being Moved**	**+**	**Meter Conversion**	**=**	**Distance in Meters**
OUTPUT	Distance washers raised _____ cm	÷	100	=	_____ meters
INPUT	Distance water fell _____ cm	÷	100	=	_____ meters
Step 3: Energy	**Force in Newtons**	**X**	**Distance in Meters**	**=**	**Energy in Joules**
OUTPUT	Force to lift washers _____ newtons	X	Distance washers raised _____ meters	=	_____ joules
INPUT	Force of falling water _____ newtons	X	Distance water fell _____ meters	=	_____ joules
Step 4: Efficiency	**Output**	**÷**	**Input**	**X**	**Efficiency in %**
	_____ joules	÷	_____ joules	X	100 = _____ %

4   Paula Schoeff et al.

COMMUNICATING IN MILLSIDE CORNERS

Professor Ipswitch has decided to hold a debate which will take place during the fair. He expects the debate to be heated, so he is looking for an impartial moderator who is willing to tackle this responsibility. The moderator needs to be well informed, so the Professor is using electronic communication – by blog, podcast, or video – by possible moderators to help him make his selection and prepare for the big event. It should be exciting!

You will participate in blog, podcast, or video conversations as you learn about hydropower and work to create a response to the Big Changes for Millside Corners Design Challenge. You will create a post about one of the topics listed below, or you may choose another topic with your teacher's approval. Your teacher will tell you when to write new posts. You will also add 2–3 comments to your previous postings. Remember that you will write and respond as your historical character.

Topics	CHOOSE ONE of These Questions	
Inventions and Design	In order to design and build something, a designer must understand the materials they are using. What materials did your team use to build the wind turbine in lesson 1 and how did this affect its design?	Designers value precision. Explain how the shape and position of the turbine blade you built in lesson 1 affected its efficiency.
Life around the Creek: Yesterday, Today, and Tomorrow	What features of Millside Corners do you value most and why?	Empire Creek runs through and along many people's property? Who should own Empire Creek?
Electrification of Millside Corners	The need for electricity has increased greatly since the building of Davis Mill in the 1700s. Do you believe our need will continue to escalate? Support your conclusion with evidence.	Provide some alternatives to converting the mill into a power plant and support your reasoning with evidence.

COMMUNICATING IN MILLSIDE CORNERS

Topics	CHOOSE ONE of These Questions	
Does Hydropower Make Sense for Millside Corners?	If Empire Creek is used to produce power, how would this impact its other uses and activities that occur on the creek?	How might the building of the hydroelectric power plant and dam impact the future of Millside Corners?
Tourism around Empire Creek	The historic Davis Mill will no longer be a part of tourism for visitors to Millside Corners if it is converted into a dam. How important is Davis Mill to the economy here?	If Davis Mill is converted into a power station, what other attractions could be developed to replace it?
Energy and the Environment	If Millside Corners converts to hydropower, the environment will be impacted. How will the new power plant and dam impact the environment around Millside Corners?	People at Millside Corners are worried that building a new hydropower plant will affect their environment, how will NOT building a power plant impact the environment?
The Role of Science in Millside Corners' Decisions	Lifelong learning is a valuable skill. How does being a lifelong learner help Millside Corner citizens make better decisions?	Science and engineering ideas can be hard to understand. How can artists, writers, and musicians help people understand science ideas?

Paula Schoeff et al.

REGIONS OF THE UNITED STATES

Figure 4.22

NATIONAL SCIENCE TEACHING ASSOCIATION

EFFICIENCY ACTIVITY RUBRIC

Name _____ Team Name_____

	Exceeds Expectations (4)	Meets Expectations (3)	Approaching Expectations (2)	Needs Improvement (1)	Incomplete (0)	Score
Observations	• Observations are accurate & complete. • Interpretations are based on experiences and observations.	• Observations are accurate & complete. • Interpretations are based only on lab observations.	• Observations are accurate, but miss important details. • Lab did not inform interpretation.	• Observations are "on the right track." • Little or no background knowledge available.	• Nonsense or blank response. • No reflection about lab is present.	
Predictions	• Clearly understands how the device or principle works. • Explains predictions and identifies reasoning.	• Understands how the device or principle works. • Can make reasonable predictions but does not explain reasoning.	• Grasps the principles of the device. • Cannot make predictions based on knowledge.	• Can draw conclusions about the device or principle. • Vaguely understands relationships or principles associated.	• Nonsense or blank response. • Does not have any knowledge necessary to complete this activity successfully.	
Pictures	• Drawings are detailed. • Detailed labels and descriptions. • Labels reflect appropriate vocabulary.	• Drawings contain several details. • All the important labels and descriptions are present. • Labels reflect a growing vocabulary.	• Drawing contains some details. • Labels drawing, but leaves out some important details. • Labels include few science terms.	• Drawing is not detailed. • Labels are incorrect, confusing, or non-technical, e.g., "circle thing-y" • No science terms.	• Unfinished drawing • No labels. • No science terms.	
Data and Results	• Tables/graphs are neat and clearly labeled. • Tables/graphs are accurate and used effectively. • Data is shown with the best method so that patterns/trends can be seen.	• Tables/graphs are labeled. • Tables/graphs are all accurate, but not helpful. • Some data is show with the best method so that some patterns can be seen.	• Tables/graphs are mislabeled. • Tables/graphs are inaccurate and difficult to interpret. • Data is unclear so that it is not possible to make clear predictions.	• Much of the data is not recorded on the tables/graphs. • It is not possible to use the tables/graphs to find a pattern. • Incorrect corrections are made due to bad data.	• No tables/graphs are visible. • No data is provided. • No predictions can be made.	
Total Score						
Comments:						

WATER WHEEL DESIGN CHALLENGE RUBRIC, PAGE 1 OF 4

Name:_____	
DEFINE: Identify the Problem	**Score**
5–6 · Student has a clear understanding of the problem and its requirements. · Student can use other ideas, concepts, or processes to construct explanations. · Student can apply knowledge to predict and solve complex problems, including those in unfamiliar situations.	
3–4 · Student can describe the problem and its requirements. · Student can recall other ideas, concepts, or processes that are identical. · Student can apply knowledge to predict and solve complex problems in familiar situations.	
1–2 · Student needs help to understand the problem. · Student may be able to recall some ideas, concepts, or processes that are identical. · Student is able to recognize and mimic examples of other solutions to the problem.	
LEARN: Brainstorm Possibilities, Choose the Best	
5–6 · All ideas are focused on solving the problem. · Student considers unlikely solutions/models. · Student uses ideas, concepts, or processes correctly to construct possible solutions.	
3–4 · Some ideas are focused on solving the problem. · Student considers multiple solutions/models. · Student mimics (copies) the best option.	
1–2 · Few ideas are focused on solving the problem. · Student uses examples or direct guidance to generate ideas for solving the problem/developing a model. · Student does not provide any original ideas.	

WATER WHEEL DESIGN CHALLENGE RUBRIC, PAGE 2 OF 4

PLAN: Research, List Needs, Plan Steps		
5–6	• Student critically investigates the problem and selects information from a broad range of sources. • Student provides a complete list of the materials needed. • Student plans and explains the steps that are used, including all of the techniques that are required.	
3–4	• Student analyzes and selects information from some recommended sources. • Student provides a list with most of the materials needed. • Student plans and explains the steps that are used with few omissions.	
1–2	• Student investigates the problem, collecting information from sources. • Student lists some of the materials needed. • Student plans and explains few of the steps that are needed.	
TRY: Follow Your Plan and Build a Model		
5–6	• Student provides detailed drawings which provide valuable information for constructing the model. • Student provides a comprehensive list of criteria for success and reasonable methods for testing each one. • Student generates a range of feasible solutions and justifies the chosen prototype.	
3–4	• Student provides drawings that provide enough information to construct a model. • Student provides some criteria for success and reasonable methods for testing them. • Student generates an alternate solution if something doesn't work right.	
1–2	• Student provides rough sketches of the design which are not very helpful. • Student provides little or no criteria for success or reasonable methods for testing. • Student generates one solution (even if a better alternative becomes available).	

Paula Schoeff et al.

WATER WHEEL DESIGN CHALLENGE RUBRIC, PAGE 3 OF 4

TEST: Try It Out! What Works? What Doesn't?		
5–6	• Student is able to manipulate materials and equipment with skill. • Student consistently adheres to plans in a precise and methodical manner. • Comprehensive testing has been done to assess the performance of the model/solution. • Test results are well documented and conclusive.	
3–4	• Student is able to manipulate materials and equipment to complete the task. • Student carries out the plan but overlooks some aspects. • The model/solution is tested against a minimum set of standards for success. • Test results are well documented and reasonable.	
1–2	• Student is not able to manipulate equipment and materials satisfactorily. • Student has not followed the specified instructions outlined in the plan. • Student has not tested the model/solution adequately. • Test results are inconclusive or misleading.	

WATER WHEEL DESIGN CHALLENGE
RUBRIC, PAGE 4 OF 4

DECIDE: Redesign to Solve Problems That Come Up	
5–6	• Student's evaluation is a thoughtful and insightful assessment based on the performance against a complete set of defined criteria for success. • The evaluation statements are justified and supported with evidence, taking into account the effectiveness and efficiency. • Realistic and innovative suggestions are made for improvement of the model/solution.	
3–4	• Student's evaluations are justified and supported with evidence taking effectiveness and efficiency of the solution/model into consideration. • Student measures performance against most of the defined criteria for success. • Student provides some realistic suggestions to address the problem or improve performance.	
1–2	• Student states expected performance. • Student considers only one or two of the defined criteria for success for the solution/model. Little or no attention was given to the effectiveness or efficiency of the performance of the model/solution.	
Total Score	
Comments:	

Remember, this is not a contest and there is no one "right" answer.
  Many solutions/models are possible.

Paula Schoeff et al.

REGIONAL MAP RUBRIC, PAGE 1 OF 2

Student Name_____   Team Name_____

	Exceeds Expectations 4	Meets Expectations 3	Approaching Expectations 2	Needs Improvement 1	Score
Title	The title tells the purpose/content of the map and is located in clear view.	The title tells the purpose/content of the map and is located in clear view.	The title tells the purpose/content of the map, but is not in clear view.	The purpose/content of the map is not present.	
Features	All major bodies of water and major landforms are present and labeled.	Most major bodies of water and landforms are present and labeled.	Some bodies of water and landforms are present and labeled.	Bodies of water and landforms are present, but are not labeled.	
Key/ Legend	All the images are in the legend and are labeled.	Most of the images are in the legend and are labeled.	Some images are in the legend and are labeled.	Images are placed on the map, but are not labeled.	
Color Choices	Appropriate colors are always used for features and resource icons.	Appropriate colors are usually used for features and resource icons.	Appropriate colors are sometimes used for features and resource icons.	Appropriate colors are not used for features or resource icons.	
Neatness	All of the features are clearly labeled and easy to read.	Most of the features are clearly labeled easy to read.	Some of the features are clearly labeled easy to read.	Few of the features are clearly labeled and easy to read.	
Accuracy	All the features and energy resources are correctly placed on the map.	Most of the features and energy resources are correctly placed on the map.	Some of the features and energy resources are correctly placed on the map.	Few of the features and energy resources are correctly placed on the map.	

REGIONAL MAP RUBRIC, PAGE 2 OF 2

	Exceeds Expectations 4	Meets Expectations 3	Approaching Expectations 2	Needs Improvement 1	Score
Spelling/ Capitalization	All words on the map are spelled and capitalized correctly.	Most words on the map are spelled and capitalized correctly.	Many words on the map are not spelled correctly, all words are capitalized.	Few words are spelled correctly, nor are they capitalized.	
Total Score					
Comments:					

Paula Schoeff et al.

ENERGY RESEARCH SLIDESHOW RUBRIC

Team Name _____   Team Score _____

Skills	Exceeds Expectations (5–6)	Meets Expectations (3–4)	Needs Improvement (1–2)	Score
Information	• Team presentation includes many relevant details with extra pieces of information. • Provides an abundance of evidence to clearly support their reasoning.	• Team presentation includes many relevant details. • Predictions to be made with evidence to support their reasoning.	• Team presentation omits many details about the assigned region. • Predictions are made without evidence to support their reasoning.	
Accuracy	• All the content is correct. • Understanding of content is obvious.	• Most of the content is correct. • Large gaps in understanding.	• Content is not correct. • Does not understand content.	
Time Management	• Manages time well. • Presentation is clear, well organized, and informative.	• Manages time adequately. • Presentation is semi-organized and informative.	• Manages time poorly. Team is frequently off task. • Presentation is difficult to follow.	
Graphics	• Images are clear. • Images are used effectively and can be used to support conclusions.	• Images are clear. • Some images are helpful but most are not necessary.	• Images are unclear. • Images distract from the presentation.	
Mechanics	• The project has 0–2 spelling errors.	• The project has 2–4 spelling errors.	• The project has 4 or more spelling errors.	
Q&A Responses	• Team responds and seeks clarification of audience questions. • Responses are full of details that clarify.	• Team responds to audience questions. • Responses are brief and incomplete.	• Team fails to respond to questions from audience. • Not able to answer many of the questions.	
Comments				

BLOG, PODCAST, OR VIDEO POST RUBRIC

Name _____   Total Score _____

	Exceeds Expectations 5–6	Meets Expectations 3–4	Needs Improvement 1–2	Score
Content	Posts show evidence of understanding and new information or a new point-of-view about the topic is introduced.	Posts show evidence of understanding and reflections provide a thought-provoking idea about the topic.	Posts show no evidence of research or insight about the topic.	
Support for Information	Posts present focused and well-supported information.	Posts present a point-of-view with little or no support.	Posts present no opinion and lack substance.	
Audience Awareness	Posts encourage dialogue and ongoing conversation and demonstrate awareness of the audience.	Posts attempt to draw peers into dialogue and ongoing conversation but reflect limited awareness of the audience	Posts do not stimulate dialogue and reflect no awareness of the audience.	
Voice	Posts are written in a style that clearly demonstrates the voice of the assigned time traveler.	Posts are written in a style that demonstrates an attempt to assume the voice of the assigned time traveler.	Posts are not written with any attempt to assume the voice of the assigned time traveler.	
Graphics and Multimedia	Selects and inserts high quality graphics and multimedia which enhance the content.	Often selects and inserts graphics and multimedia which enhance the content.	Does not insert any graphics or uses low quality graphics and multimedia which do not enhance the content.	
	Provides captions and cites sources for all images and multimedia content.	Provides captions and cites sources for most images and multimedia content.	Does not cite any image or multimedia sources nor use captions to describe the content.	
Grammar and Spelling	Posts are free of spelling or grammar errors.	Posts have few spelling or grammar errors.	Posts have many spelling or grammar errors.	

Comments:

Lesson Plan 3:
Under Pressure: Water Pressure and Dams

In this lesson, students explore types of dams and make a decision about which type would be best for Millside Corners. Students work in teams to investigate water pressure and experiment with different shapes and sizes of dams. Teams' findings will inform their decisions for the Big Changes for Millside Corners Design Challenge in Lesson 4.

ESSENTIAL QUESTIONS

- How does the height of a dam affect the pressure of water being released through the outlets?

- Why is a dam thicker at the bottom than at the top?

- How is a turbine different than a water wheel?

- Why is it important to make use of renewable resources when generating electricity?

- What are some ways that citizens help educate the public about effective use of resources?

ESTABLISHED GOALS AND OBJECTIVES

At the conclusion of this lesson, students will be able to do the following:

- Describe water pressure and apply their understanding to predict the direction that water will flow in a pipe or field

- Identify the parts of a dam

- Apply the EDP to design a model of a dam

- Recognize that water pressure increases with water depth

- Identify effects that dams and reservoirs may have on natural habitats

- Apply their understanding of energy sources to create an infographic to explain the importance of utilizing renewable energy

- Apply their understanding of energy sources to create an opinion essay

- Evaluate renewable energy resources from the perspective of an historical figure and communicate these ideas in writing.

TIME REQUIRED

6 days (approximately 45 minutes each day; see Table 3.8)

MATERIALS

Required Materials for Lesson 3

- STEM Research Notebooks

- Computer with Internet access for playing online simulation and Internet blogging activity

- Books:

  - *Paddle to the Sea* by Holling C. Holling

  - *Canals and Dams: Investigate Feats of Engineering* by Donna Latham [ISBN-13: 978–1619301658]

- Slideshow: Dams and Design – www.routledge.com/9781032618074

- Handouts and resources (attached at the end of Lesson 3)

  - Water Pressure Activity student handout

  - Build a Dam Design Challenge student handout

  - EDP Applied to the Dam Design Challenge student handout

  - OREO Writing Template student handout

- Rubrics (attached at the end of Lesson 3)

  - Water Pressure Activity Rubric

  - Opinion Writing Rubric

  - Energy Infographic Rubric

Additional Materials for Water Pressure Lab (for each team of 3–4 students unless otherwise noted)

- 2-liter soda bottle w/ lid, half filled with water (1 per class)

- bucket or bin

- access to water

- 3 tall disposable cups (24 oz)

- 3″ – 4″ framing nail

- #2 pencil

- watertight bin

- 30 cm ruler

- 18" strip of masking tape

- pitcher or water bottle to fill the cups

- waterproof grease pen or marker (optional)

Additional Materials for Dam Building Design Challenge (for each team of 3–4 students unless otherwise noted)

- 2 pounds of sand

- 2 pounds of gravel

- a waterproof bin

- empty 2-liter soda bottles

- access to water (4 liters per test)

- waterproof bag that can hold 4 liters of water

- an assortment of building materials: cardboard, tape, craft sticks, straws, modeling clay, wire, twine, plastic sheeting, etc.

Additional Materials for Energy Infographic Activity (for each student)

- paper

- ruler

- colored pencils

- black, fine-tip marker

SAFETY NOTES

1. Remind students that personal protective equipment (safety glasses or goggles, aprons, and gloves) must be worn during the setup, hands-on, and takedown segments of activities.

2. Students should use caution when handling scissors as the sharp points and blades can cut or puncture skin.

3. Tell students to be careful when handling containers. Cut plastic may have sharp edges, which can cut or puncture skin. Plastic can break and cut skin.

4. Immediately wipe up any spilled water to avoid a slip-and-fall hazard.

CONTENT STANDARDS AND KEY VOCABULARY

Table 4.8 lists the content standards from the *NGSS, CCSS,* and the Framework for 21st Century Learning that this lesson addresses, and Table 4.9 presents the key vocabulary. Vocabulary terms are provided for both teacher and student use. Teachers may choose to introduce some or all of the terms to students.

Table 4.8 Content Standards Addressed in STEM Road Map Module Lesson 3

NEXT GENERATION SCIENCE STANDARDS
PERFORMANCE OBJECTIVES
- 4-ESS3-1. Obtain and combine information to describe that energy and fuels are derived from natural resources and their uses affect the environment.
- 4-PS3-2. Make observations to provide evidence that energy can be transferred from place to place by sound, light, heat, and electrical currents.
- 4-PS3–4. Apply scientific ideas to design, test, and refine a device that converts energy from one form to another.

DISCIPLINARY CORE IDEAS
ESS3.A: Natural Resources
- Energy and fuels that humans use are derived from natural sources, and their use affects the environment in multiple ways. Some resources are renewable over time, and others are not.
PS3.A: Definitions of Energy
- Energy can be moved from place to place by mobbing objects or through sound, light, or electric currents.
PS3.B: Conservation of Energy and Energy Transfer
- Energy is present whenever there are moving objects, sound, light, or heat. When objects collide, energy can be transferred from one object to another, thereby changing their motion. In such collisions, some energy is typically also transferred to the surrounding air; as a result, the air gets heated and sound is produced.
- Energy can also be transferred from place to place by electric currents, which can then be used locally to produce motion, sound, heat, or light. The currents may have been produced to being with by transforming the energy of motion into electrical energy.
PS3.D: Energy in Chemical Processes and Everyday Life
- The expression "produce energy" typically refers to the conservation of stored energy into a desired form for practical use.

CROSSCUTTING CONCEPTS
Cause and Effect
- Cause and effect relationships are routinely identified and used to explain change.

Table 4.8 (*continued*)

Energy and Matter
- Energy can be transferred in various ways and between objects.

Systems and System Models
- A system can be described in terms of its components and their interactions.

SCIENCE AND ENGINEERING PRACTICES

Asking Questions and Defining Problems
- Ask questions that can be investigated and predict reasonable outcomes based on patterns such as cause and effect relationships.

Developing and Using Models
- Develop a model to describe phenomena.
- Use a model to test interactions concerning the functioning of a natural system.

Planning and Carrying Out Investigations
- Make observations to produce data to serve as the basis for evidence for an explanation of a phenomenon or test a design solution.

Constructing Explanations and Designing Solutions
- Identify the evidence that supports particular points in an explanation.
- Use evidence (e.g., measurements, observations, patterns) to construct an explanation.
- Generate and compare multiple solutions to a problem based on how well they meet the criteria and constraints of the design solution.
- Apply scientific ideas to solve design problems.

Obtaining, Evaluating, and Communicating Information
- Obtain and combine information from books and other reliable media to explain phenomena.

COMMON CORE STATE STANDARDS FOR MATHEMATICS

MATHEMATICAL PRACTICES
- 4.MP1. Make sense of problems and persevere in solving them.
- 4.MP2. Reason abstractly and quantitatively.
- 4.MP3. Construct viable arguments and critique the reasoning of others.
- 4.MP4. Model with mathematics.
- 4.MP5. Use appropriate tools strategically.
- 4.MP6. Attend to precision.

MATHEMATICAL CONTENT
- 4.MD.A.2. Use the four operations to solve word problems involving distances, intervals of time, liquid volumes, masses of objects, and money, including problems involving simple fractions or decimals, and problems that require expressing measurements given in a larger unit in terms of a smaller unit. Represent measurement quantities using diagrams such as number line diagrams that feature a measurement scale.
- 4.MD.B.4. Make a line plot to display a data set of measurements in fractions of a unit (1/2, 1/4, 1/8). Solve problems involving addition and subtraction of fractions by using information presented in line plots.
- 4.MD.C.5. Recognize angles as geometric shapes that are formed wherever two rays share a common endpoint, and understand concepts of angle measurement.

Table 4.8 (*continued*)

COMMON CORE STATE STANDARDS FOR ENGLISH LANGUAGE ARTS

READING STANDARDS

- RI.4.1. Refer to details and examples in a text when explaining what the text says explicitly and when drawing inferences from the text.
- RI.4.2. Determine the main idea of a text and explain how it is supported by key details, summarize the text.
- RI.4.3. Explain events, procedures, ideas, or concepts in a historical, scientific or technical text, including what happened and why, based on specific information in the text.
- RI.4.4. Determine the meaning of general academic and domain-specific words or phrases in a text relevant to a grade 4 topic or subject area.
- RI.4.6. Compare and contrast a firsthand and secondhand account of the same event or topic; describe the differences in focus and the information provided.
- RI.4.7. Interpret information presented visually, orally, or quantitatively (e.g., in charts, graphs, diagrams, time lines, animations, or interactive elements on Web pages) and explain how the information contributes to an understanding of the text in which it appears.
- RI.4.9. Integrate information from two texts on the same topic in order to write or speak about the subject knowledgeably.

WRITING STANDARDS

- W.4.2. Write informative/explanatory texts to examine a topic and convey ideas and information clearly.
- W.4.6. With some guidance and support from adults, use technology, including the Internet, to produce and publish writing as well as to interact and collaborate with others; demonstrate sufficient command of keyboarding skills to type a minimum of one page in a single sitting.
- W.4.7. Conduct short research projects that build knowledge through investigation of different aspects of a topic.
- W.4.8. Recall relevant information from experiences or gather relevant information from print and digital sources; take notes and categorize information, and provide a list of sources.
- W.4.9. Draw evidence from literary or informational texts to support analysis, reflection, and research.

SPEAKING AND LISTENING STANDARDS

- SL.4.1. Engage effectively in a range of collaborative discussions (one-on-one, in groups, and teacher-led) with diverse partners on *grade 4 topics and texts*, building on others' ideas and expressing their own clearly.
- SL.4.4. Report on a topic or text, tell a story, or recount an experience in an organized manner, using appropriate facts and relevant, descriptive details to support main ideas or themes; speak clearly at an understandable pace.
- SL.4.5. Add audio recordings and visual displays to presentations when appropriate to enhance the development of main ideas or themes.

Table 4.8 (*continued*)

FRAMEWORK FOR 21ST CENTURY LEARNING
• Interdisciplinary Themes (financial, economic, & business literacy; environmental literacy) • Learning and Innovation Skills • Information, Media & Technology Skills • Life and Career Skills

Table 4.9 Key Vocabulary in Lesson 3

Key Vocabulary	Definition
altitude	height above sea level
arch dam	tall concrete dam built for narrow valleys with rock walls and held in place by the canyon walls
beaver dam	short mud and stick dam built by beavers in ponds and streams and held in place by anchor sticks
buttress dam	large concrete dam with buttress structures built in valleys with dirt walls and held in place by its own weight
depth	a measurement from top to bottom
embankment dam	short earthen dam built for wide valleys with dirt walls and held in place by its own weight
equalize	the tendency of forces in a system to move into balance
gravity dam	large concrete dam used in wide valleys and held in place by its own weight
head	in a hydropower system, difference in elevation between water behind the dam and water entering the turbine
hydrostatic pressure	the pressure exerted by fluid due to the force of gravity
infographic	a visual representation of information using charts, graphs, or images with little or no text
inlet	a place or opening for letting a fluid into a container or reservoir
mechanical	the energy associated with the motion and position of an object (the sum of K.E. and P.E.)
outlet	a place or opening for letting a fluid out of a container or reservoir
pressure	a force pressing steadily against a surface or object
reservoir	a man-made lake or container for collecting and storing water
stakeholder	a person who has an interest in a decision and who is affected by and cares about how it turns out
structure	an object built from more than one part, put together in a certain way

TEACHER BACKGROUND INFORMATION

In this lesson, students investigate forces in the standing water behind a dam. Students will investigate water pressure and structural features of dams that enable them to stand up to that pressure.

Hydrostatic Pressure

Water pressure is a type of hydrostatic pressure – the pressure exerted by a fluid due to gravity. The pressure in a fluid comes from the mass of the fluid above, pressing downward. This principle holds true even in very irregularly shaped bodies of water. The interactive *Under Pressure* simulation on the Phet website at https://phet.colorado.edu/en/simulations/under-pressure illustrates this principle.

Students will discover in the Water Pressure Activity that pressure increases as depth below the surface increases. At a given depth below the surface, the pressure is the same throughout the body of water. This is true regardless of the shape or size of the body of water. The water pressure three meters below the surface of Empire Reservoir or three meters below the surface of the local swimming pool diving tank is virtually the same. In contrast, pressure at three meters is substantially different than the pressure at a depth of two meters, one meter, or ten meters.

Blaise Pascal, a 17th century French scientist, is credited with demonstrating that pressure exerted anywhere in a fluid like water is transmitted equally in all directions. He demonstrated this by bursting a wooden barrel by adding water to a tall, narrow tube inserted in the lid. Though the weight of the water in the tube was far less than that of the water in the barrel, the extreme height of the surface of the water in the tube (10 meters) added so much pressure that the barrel burst at the base. This phenomenon, known as Pascal's law, is often used in the design of hydropower systems.

Figure 4.23 below shows the basic design of a dam that is used to create hydroelectric power by employing hydrostatic pressure. A turbine is connected to the dam by a pipe called a penstock tube. The turbine is some distance away from the dam and located downhill from the dam. Because the penstock is connected to the reservoir, the pressure at the turbine is the sum of the pressure at the foot of the dam plus the vertical distance between the dam and the turbine. In effect, pressure at the turbine is the same as if the dam was 60 meters high! With more pressure comes the potential to generate more electricity. This is why the Buckeye University researchers (introduced in Lesson 1) recommend that the power plant be located at the Davis Mill site, rather than at the foot of Empire Reservoir Dam since the additional vertical distance provides substantially more hydrostatic pressure to drive generators.

Figure 4.23 Dam for hydroelectric power

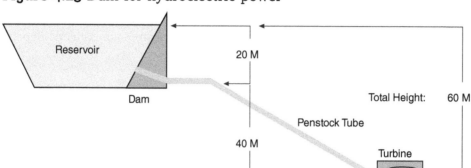

Photo credit: Pandaia Projects LLC. See Internet Resources section for link to licensing information.

Dam Design

Background for dam design is provided in the book *Canals and Dams* listed in the Materials section of this lesson (see p. XX). Additional information about dams can be found on the PBS Building Big Site at www.pbs.org/wgbh/buildingbig/dam/.

Opinion Writing

In preparation for the debate students will participate in later in the module, students will research hydroelectric power and other alternatives for Millside Corners. Using what they learn, students will write a five-paragraph opinion paper to help them organize their ideas and gather support for their opinion.

One strategy for writing opinion papers is called the OREO strategy, where the acronym OREO is used as follows:

- O = Write an introduction – clearly state your opinion.

- R = Give 2–3 reasons why you hold this opinion.

- E = Provide 2–3 examples to support these reasons, providing details.

- O = Opinion is restated your conclusions with enthusiasm.

Writing an opinion essay the OREO way provides a simple template that will offer your students an opportunity to research to find evidence to support their viewpoints and then synthesize their findings. A template for OREO writing is provided in the resources at the end of this lesson.

4

Infographics

Students will create an energy infographic in this lesson. An infographic (information graphic) presents information, data, or knowledge in a visual form. These graphics are often used to illustrate and explain complex information in an engaging way that is not overwhelming, The task of creating an infographic requires that students synthesize their learning. The following is an overview of steps in creating an infographic:

1. Think of an idea – Make a list of possible ideas for your infographic.

2. Create a flowchart – This is your outline or draft.

3. Create a color scheme – Use eye-friendly colors such as pastels and bright colors.

4. Choose eye-catching graphics – People like visuals more than text.

5. Research – Use a variety of good sources.

6. Provide facts and conclusions – Create graphs and tables to visually show your statistics. Make it simple.

7. Edit, edit, and edit! – Review everything. Try to create a story.

The following are additional tips for creating effective Infographics:

- Use eye-catching colors and visuals

- Use pie charts, pictorial charts, or bar graphs to present information.

- A word picture such as a Wordle™ can be used to introduce key terms (www.wordle.net/).

- Change the direction or angle of the text and/or images to divide the page into sections.

- Utilize a variety of different font styles.

For more information about using infographics in the classroom, see www.schrockguide.net/infographics-as-an-assessment.html.

COMMON MISCONCEPTIONS

Students will have various types of prior knowledge about the concepts introduced in this lesson. Table 4.10 outlines some common misconceptions students may have concerning these concepts. Because of the breadth of students' experiences, it is not possible to anticipate every misconception that students may bring as they approach

Table 4.10 Common Misconceptions about the Concepts in Lesson 3

Topic	Student Misconception	Explanation
Geology	Human activities cannot affect geological processes like the flow of water	Humans can change the flow of water in rivers by diverting the flow of water using structures such as dams, floodgates, and levees.
	Rivers flow from north to south	Rivers flow from the source (higher elevation) to the mouth (lower elevation); this is sometimes, but not always, in a north to south direction.

this lesson. Incorrect or inaccurate prior understanding of concepts can influence student learning in the future, however, so it is important to be alert to misconceptions such as those presented in the table.

PREPARATION FOR LESSON 3

Review the Teacher Background Information provided, assemble the materials for the lesson, make copies of the student handouts, and preview the slideshow and videos recommended in the Learning Plan Components section below.

Prepare Water Pressure stations, one for each team, with the materials listed in the materials list. Make sure that teams have access to water.

Paddle to the Sea is a Caldecott Honor Book written in 1941 that tells the story of a model boat and its journey from Lake Nipigon, Canada to the Atlantic Ocean through the Great Lakes and the St. Lawrence River. This book is incorporated into the Introductory Activity/Engagement section of this lesson as an illustration of water's relentless pursuit of moving to ever lower levels. Since the book is 64 pages long you may wish to substitute a video adaption of the book rather than reading it aloud. A 28-minute video created for the National Film Board of Canada is available at www.nfb.ca/film/paddle_to_the_sea.

Be prepared to provide examples of infographics for students. You may wish to access examples from the Internet from a website about creating infographics such as www.schrockguide.net/infographics-as-an-assessment.html, by conducting an Internet search using a search term such as "infographics for elementary students" or you may wish to use a book such as *Energy and Waves through Infographics* by Rebecca Rowell to provide examples.

Visit your local library to compile a collection of nonfiction books that can be used to discuss hydroelectric plants and dams and the effects of water pressure. There may be some good fiction books that address renewable resources as well. The librarian may put a collection together for you if you call ahead.

LEARNING PLAN COMPONENTS
Introductory Activity/Engagement

Connection to the Challenge: Begin each day of this lesson by directing students' attention to the module challenge, Big Changes for Millside Corners Design Challenge. Hold a brief class discussion each day of how students' learning in the previous days' lessons contributed to their ability to complete the challenge. You may wish to create a class list of key ideas on chart paper.

Science Class and Social Studies and Mathematics, ELA, and Social Studies Connections: Have students respond to the following prompts in their STEM Research Notebooks:

- Compare and contrast a river and an ocean

- Mount Everest is the highest mountain in the world with an altitude of 8,850 meters. What is meant by the term altitude?

After students have answered these questions, have several students share their responses and hold a class discussion about the prompts, recording students' ideas on chart paper.

Next, read aloud the book *Paddle to the Sea* by Holling C. Holling or show the video adaptation of the book found at www.nfb.ca/film/paddle_to_the_sea. After reading the book or watching the video, hold a class discussion, asking questions such as:

- How did the little boat get to the water?

- When snow melts, where does it go?

- Describe a time in the video when the boat was moving fast.

  - What was the water like?

  - Why was it moving so fast?

- Describe a time in the video when the water was moving slowly.

  - What was the water like?

  - What makes you think the water was moving?

- The boat in the video, always moved with the water. Describe a time when you were in a boat that was moving against the flow of water.

  - What made the boat you were in move against the flow?

  - Which takes more energy, to move with the flow of water or against it? Why?

- Describe a part of the story where water had a large amount of energy.

  - Where did the energy come from?

- Arrange these descriptions of moving water by the amount of energy of the movement. What determines how much force moving water has? (Hint: total mass of water times the distance it falls)

  - A raindrop falling from a cloud

  - A giant waterfall falling hundreds of feet

  - Water running along the street during a strong rain

  - A broad river flowing slowly through an open field

  - A tear running down your cheek

Activity/Exploration

Science Class and Mathematics and Social Studies Connections: Students will explore water pressure in the Water Pressure Activity and will apply the EDP to create a dam model in the Build a Dam Design Challenge.

Ask students to name some reasons that people build dams, creating a class list of students' responses. Next, ask students for their ideas about how dams could impact the environment, recording students' responses on chart paper.

Next, have students explore dams by reviewing (either individually or as a class) a website such as PBS's "Dam Basics" at https://www.pbs.org/wgbh/buildingbig/dam/basics.html. Have students take notes about their learning in their STEM Research Notebooks. Hold a class discussion about what students learned about dams.

Introduce the concept of water pressure with a discussion of the term pressure. The term pressure comes from the word press. Pressure means a force pressing steadily against a surface or object. Remind students that force is a push or a pull. Work need not be done for pressure to be present. Pressure is a form of potential energy since it is the capacity to do work.

Tell students to pretend that they won a goldfish at the school fair and are taking the goldfish home in in a baggie filled with water. The baggie has a teeny tiny hole in it, but the hole is on the top of the baggie, just below where the baggie is tied off. Tell students to imagine that they decide to carry the bag home in their backpacks. Ask students what happens and why, relating their ideas to the concept of water pressure. An option is to have students explore water pressure using a simulation such as that found at https://phet.colorado.edu/en/simulations/under-pressure. Tell students that they will explore water pressure in the Water Pressure Activity.

Water Pressure Activity

Introduce the activity by holding a class discussion, asking students the following questions:

- What are we doing when we blow up a balloon or pump up a bike tire?

- Why does water always flow downstream?

- Is there a circumstance when a water surface can be slanted downhill? *Possible accurate answers would include:*

  - *a frozen glacier running down the side of a mountain*

  - *water flowing in an inclined trough or pipe*

Illustrate pressure by blowing up a balloon. Have students predict what will happen as you continue to blow into the balloon. Point out to students that air pressure holds the balloon open and causes the walls to stretch. Ask the students for their ideas about the pressure inside the balloon, asking:

- Is the air pressure same throughout the balloon?

- Does the air push more on one side of the balloon than on another?

Press on the sides of the balloon to illustrate that when you add pressure by squeezing, the balloon adjusts its shape to equalize pressure on the inside. Use this property to guide the students to the conclusion that air pressure is the same throughout the balloon.

Next, show students the partially filled 2-liter bottle. Rotate the bottle end to end and have students make observations about the behavior of the water. Hold the bottle sideways and tilt just a little toward one end to illustrate that no matter how hard you try you cannot keep the water from running downhill. Remind students that water always seeks the lowest level by relating this idea to the *Paddle to the Sea* book or video and ask students the following questions:

- How did the little boat get from the mountains to the sea?

- Which was higher, the mountain or the sea?

- Paddle floated on many big lakes in his journey to the sea. If water always flows downhill, does that mean the surface of the lakes was tilted like a slide?

Next, remove the lid from the 2-liter bottle and tilt the bottle by degrees toward an empty bucket or bin until the water level is just below the opening. Introduce the term *outlet* as a place or opening for letting a fluid out of a container. Tilt the bottle enough for water to begin flowing out of the bottle. Emphasize to students water will

always flow through the outlet when the level of the outlet is below the level of the water in the container. Remind students that work happens when force overcomes resistance and moves something. The water is clearly moving. Ask students to name the forces involved in the water exiting the bottle through the outlet, guiding students to understand that gravity is the force moving the water.

Next, ask students what they think about the pressure that water has when in the soda bottle asking whether it is the same throughout the container as was the air pressure in the balloon. Refill the bottle, and point to various places down the side below the level of the water, questioning students whether the pressure of the water against the bottle is the same at each place. Tell students that in this activity they will discover how water behaves in a container and explain that water's behavior will be essentially the same whether the "container" is Lake Superior, Empire Reservoir, or a 2-liter soda bottle.

Ask students if they have experienced the sensation of pressure on their ears when swimming under water. Tell students that this is because with increased depth under water there is greater pressure. This principle is essential in the design of dams, especially if the dam will be used for hydropower.

Distribute the Water Pressure Activity student handouts to each student. Have each student team follow the directions on the handout.

Build A Dam Design Challenge

Hold a class discussion about structure and function using the following discussion prompts:

- There is an old saying, "A chain is only as strong as its weakest link." What does this mean and how could it apply to building a dam?

- Another famous saying comes from Louis Sullivan, an American architect who designed the first skyscraper, "Form ever follows function." What do you think Mr. Sullivan meant by this?

- What is meant by the term structure? (Give examples of some structures large and small, simple and complex. As students discuss their understanding of the term guide them to realize that structures are built to serve a specific purpose.)

- Share the formal definition for structure (*an object built from more than one part, put together in a certain way*). Ask the students about the characteristics or parts needed to build a structure that holds back water in a river or stream.

Tell students that in this activity, they will work in teams to build a model of a dam in order to acquaint them with various kinds of dam structures. Tell students that

their teams will use an assortment of craft materials to build a dam model that meets the following requirements:

- must have a sand or gravel layer on the floor of the bin

- must be able to hold back four liters of water

- must have a movable gate to allow water to pass through.

Share the *Dams and Designs* slide presentation, found at www.routledge.com/ 9781032618074 with students. As each new style of dam is introduced, prompt students to look for the geometric shapes in the design.

Next, ask students to provide ideas about the type of components and materials that may go into building a dam. Remind them that dams are among the largest man-made objects on earth. Have students make observations about the sites in the dam photos in the slideshow. Stress that different sites call for different types of dams; for example, an embankment dam would be quickly washed away in a narrow canyon more suited for an arch dam.

Review the "Building Big: The Physics of Dams" section of the book *Canals and Dams: Investigate Feats of Engineering* with the class.

Distribute the Build a Dam Design Challenge student handout to each student and an EDP Applied to the Dam Design Challenge handout to each team. Student teams will proceed through each step of the EDP as they complete the challenge:

Define: The problem teams will solve is to build an embankment dam which can hold back four liters of water. The site must have a sand and/or gravel bed. The dam must have at least one outlet which can open and shut to let water through.

Learn: The teams have been given some common craft materials: cardboard, tape, craft sticks, straws, modeling clay, wire, twine, plastic sheeting, etc. Teams may need additional materials depending on their design choices. Encourage teams to brainstorm about how to use these materials to build their site and their dam.

Plan: Two of the main phases of a structural project are site and structure.

- Students should plan the site to be able to hold four liters of water at a reasonable depth. Remind students that this is equivalent to two 2-liter soda bottles.

- Students should plan the dam structure with a focus on basic geometric shapes and the materials which will be best suited to those structural elements.

Try: Once the site is ready teams will begin building a prototype for the dam. Sometimes it becomes clear that the original ideas do not work. Encourage teams to tweak their designs until the model works.

Test: Have students test their dams without getting their models wet. This can be done by filling a plastic bag with water to determine the dam's stability without getting the site wet by applying force to their dam similar to that which will be exerted by the water. Remind the teams of their discoveries about water pressure in relation to depth. What holds the water back at the top of the dam may be insufficient at the bottom of the dam. Stress that they should not introduce water in their testing until they have a way to remove it from their models.

Decide: As testing reveals flaws in materials or construction, teams should improve their designs. If teams cannot get their dams to hold water at the base, remind them that real dams have foundations below the floor of the river or stream. If they cannot get the dam to hold back water, they should figure out a way to seal the face of the dam to the floor of the bin.

Explanation

Science Class and Mathematics Connection: Have each team share its dam designs with another team. Each team should give its partner team feedback on their model. Give students time to make modifications to their models based upon feedback and note the feedback they received and any modifications they made in their STEM Research Notebooks. Hold a class discussion about how the dams might have behaved differently with a greater or smaller volume of water.

ELA and Social Studies Connections: Continue with students' blogging, podcasting, or video creation activities. Hold a class discussion about the posts, asking students the following questions:

- What posts have you read this week which gave you new ideas or helped you solve a problem?

- If you use someone else's idea in a post, why is it a good idea to give them credit?

- If you were going to make rules for a discussion about a blog, podcast, or video, what would they be?

Have students continue to create posts throughout this lesson at the frequency you decided upon. Remind students that Professor Ipswitch will use their posts to determine who will be a good moderator for the debate.

To prepare for the debate in Lesson 4, hold a class discussion about debates, asking students the following questions:

- What is meant by the terms *pros* and *cons* when talking about making choices?

- Is a debate a good way to make a decision? Are there decisions which should not be made by debating?

- People in Millside Corners are talking about making a decision on the hydropower question. Do you think some of the people in Millside Corners are teaming up to have the decision go their way? What kinds of groups might be forming?

Discuss the term *stakeholder*. Ask students to identify the stakeholders in the Empire Creek decision. Ask them to consider which of the stakeholders their character would most likely support.

Review the highlights from the student's energy map presentations in Lesson 2. Allow students to identify some of the pros and cons to using renewable energy that they encountered in their research.

Have students write a sentence on a sheet of paper to answer the following question: *Should Millside Corners convert Davis Mill into a hydroelectric power plant?* Collect the papers and have student volunteers help you read the statements aloud and record a tally of those who support the conversion and those who do not, as a baseline for the debate. Remind students that these are opinions; there is no one right answer.

Explain to students that you will be dividing the class into two teams for the debate. If the negative and affirmative answers are fairly equal, students can work in these groups for the debate; if they are not evenly matched, assign students to take sides of the debate. Use this opportunity to explain to students that even if they do not personally support a topic they can still debate for it.

To prepare for the debate, student teams will conduct research and each student will write an opinion essay. Each team will also create an energy infographic poster. To introduce the opinion essay, tell students that they will write an essay the OREO way. Tell students that this helps them to remember the structure for their essays using the initials OREO (Opinion, Reason, Examples, Opinion). Pass out the OREO Writing Template student handout to each student and review the components.

Hold a class discussion about the difference between an opinion and a fact, asking students to name examples of each. Review the following steps of writing an opinion essay with students:

Step 1. Begin by restating the question in your own words. [Do you think Millside Corners should convert Davis Mill into a hydroelectric power plant?]

Step 2.   Write a sentence to clearly state your opinion on the question. (O)

Step 3.   Write a sentence that explains a reason for your opinion. (R)

Step 4.   Give an example/evidence for your opinion. (E)

Step 5.   Conclude the paragraph with a sentence that reinforces or repeats your opinion. (O)

Remind students that the more reasons and examples they include in their essays, the better prepared they will be for the debate. Remind students there are no right or wrong opinions, but it is important that opinions be supported with accurate facts and not mere opinions.

Have students conduct research to find information and examples to support their opinions. Encourage them to watch for statistics, interesting pictures, and quotes about renewable energy that they can use on the energy infographic posters they will create in the Elaboration/Application of Knowledge section of the lesson.

Elaboration/Application of Knowledge

Science Class and Mathematics, ELA, and Social Studies Connections: Tell students that they will work in their teams to create energy infographics using their learning about renewable energy sources. Introduce infographics by asking students the following questions:

- What is meant by the expression "A picture is worth a thousand words"?

- What are some examples of pictures that are meaningful to you or that hold meaning for many people?

- How can pictures and facts be combined to communicate information?

Show students the examples of infographics you prepared (see Preparation for Lesson 3, p. XX). Distribute the Infographic Rubric to each student and review the criteria so that students understand the traits of effective infographics.

Energy Infographic

Discuss the steps used to creating an infographic and discuss each step (see Teacher Background, p. XX). Tell students that the purpose of the infographic they will create is to promote using renewable energy. Tell students that they should demonstrate with their infographics that nonrenewable energy sources such as coal and natural gas and oil can be used up and renewable resources such as sun air, and water are good alternatives. Remind students that they should provide evidence to support their ideas. Teams may wish to focus on a single renewable resource or on several in their infographics.

After teams have created their infographics, post them on the classroom wall and have student teams view all infographics. Hold a class discussion about what students learned from the infographics and what techniques (e.g., images, graphs) they found particularly impactful.

Evaluation/Assessment

Students may be assessed on the following performance tasks and other measures listed.

Performance Tasks

- Water Pressure Activity
- Dam Design Challenge
- OREO opinion essay
- Energy Infographic poster
- Blog, podcast, or video

Other Measures

- Teacher observations
- STEM Research Notebook entries
- Student participation in teams

INTERNET RESOURCES

- Water pressure simulation: https://phet.colorado.edu/en/simulations/under-pressure
- PBS dam information: www.pbs.org/wgbh/buildingbig/dam/
- Wordle™: www.wordle.net/
- Infographics resource: www.schrockguide.net/infographics-as-an-assessment.html
- *Paddle to the Sea* video: www.nfb.ca/film/paddle_to_the_sea

4   Paula Schoeff et al.

WATER PRESSURE ACTIVITY

Materials

Each team will need 3 tall disposable cups (24 oz), 3" – 4" framing nail, pencil, a watertight bin, 30 cm ruler, 18" strip of masking tape, pitcher or water bottle to fill the cups, waterproof grease pen or marker (optional)

Procedure

1. **Prepare the Cups:** Prepare three cups for the investigation.

   - Mark a fill line on the INSIDE of each cup with the marker. (Use the ruler to mark 4–5 dots on the inside of the cup, 3 cm from the top of the cup, then connect the dots.) The fill line should be in the same location for each cup, 3 cm from the top rim.

   - Using a nail, punch one outlet hole in each cup as described below. Enlarge the holes with a pencil. Note that the holes should be snug around the pencil.

     - *Hole locations*: 1) near the bottom of the cup; 2) ⅓ of the distance from the bottom of the cup to the fill line; 3) ⅔ of the distance from the bottom of the cup to the fill line.

   - Measure the distance from the outlet to the fill line in inches or centimeters. This measurement is the "depth" since it shows how far the outlet is located below the fill line.

   - Mark the depth measurement on the side of each cup.

   - List the depths for the cups in the Depth column of the Water Pressure Data Table.

2. **Position the Cup:** Place the cup so it rests above the bin, with the bottom edge of the cup about level with the top edge of the bin and slightly overhanging the top edge of the bin – this is the "cup zone."

3. **Prepare the Bin:** Make sure there is plenty of free room inside the bin in front of the cup zone. Attach a ruler along the bottom of the bin leading straight out from the cup zone.

4. **Prepare Data Collection Sheet:** Examine each cup. Make predictions about where the water will land when released into the bin from each of the cups by ranking the cups (1 = furthest, 2 = middle, 3 = least far). Record these predictions on the on the Water Pressure Data Table.

WATER PRESSURE ACTIVITY

Water Pressure Data Table

Depth distance from fill line to hole	Predicted Rank	Actual Rank	Water Distance furthest the water traveled			
			Trial 1	Trial 2	Trial 3	Average

5. **Prepare the Line Plot Graph:** Create a graph to record your results to help you find a pattern if one is present.

   - Label the vertical axis, "Depth" and the horizontal axis, "Water Distance."

   - Mark off a scale on the left and bottom with suitable distances.

6. **Data Gathering:** Fill the cup to the fill line while plugging the outlet with the pencil.

   - Place the cup in the cup zone with the outlet positioned over the bin.

   - Unblock the outlet allowing the water to shoot out into the bin.

   - Mark the furthest place where water lands on the tape using a piece of masking tape or the grease marker.

   - Observe the behavior of the water as it drains through the outlet. Pour the water in the bucket or pitcher.

   - Repeat three times for each cup and average the results. Make sure the cup is always filled to the fill line. Make sure the cup is always placed in the same way in the cup zone for each trial.

   - Record data on the data collection sheet and plot the final average on the line plot graph.

4 Paula Schoeff et al.

WATER PRESSURE ACTIVITY

7. **STEM Research Notebook:** Each person should record data and observations about the activity in your STEM Research Notebooks.

   - Include a sketch of the cups and the part of the bin where the testing was done.

   - Be sure to label the parts and provide a description of the test you performed.

   - Include reflections about the results for the various depths.

   - Add a sketch of the graph and your observations about the data points.

8. **Reflection Questions:** answer these questions in your STEM Research Notebooks.

   - If the water shoots farther from one outlet than another, what can you conclude about the water pressure at that outlet?

   - How does water pressure change with depth?

   - What did you notice about the water stream as water drained from the cup?

   - Why do you think towns often store water in large tanks high off the ground like the picture below?

   - If the town builds a new tower that is shorter, how will water pressure be affected?

Figure 4.24

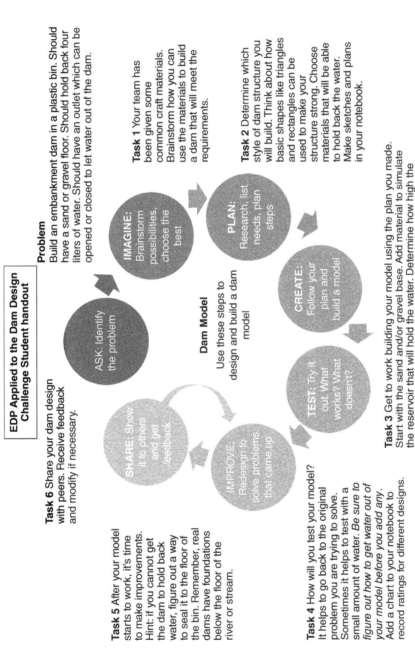

EDP Applied to the Dam Design
Challenge Student handout

Problem
Build an embankment dam in a plastic bin. Should
have a sand or gravel floor. Should hold back four
liters of water. Should have an outlet which can be
opened or closed to let water out of the dam.

Task 1 Your team has
been given some
common craft materials.
Brainstorm how you can
use the materials to build
a dam that will meet the
requirements.

Task 2 Determine which
style of dam structure you
will build. Think about how
basic shapes like triangles
and rectangles can be
used to make your
structure strong. Choose
materials that will be able
to hold back the water.
Make sketches and plans
in your notebook.

IMAGINE:
Brainstorm
possibilities,
choose the
best

PLAN:
Research, list
needs, plan
steps

ASK: Identify
the problem

Dam Model
Use these steps to
design and build a dam
model

CREATE:
Follow your
plan and
build a model

TEST: Try it
out. What
works? What
doesn't?

SHARE: Show
it to others
and get
feedback

IMPROVE:
Redesign to
solve problems
that came up

Task 3 Get to work building your model using the plan you made.
Start with the sand and/or gravel base. Add material to simulate
the reservoir that will hold the water. Determine how high the
dam needs to be to hold 4 liters of water.

Task 6 Share your dam design
with peers. Receive feedback
and modify if necessary.

Task 5 After your model
starts to work, it's time
to make improvements.
Hint: if you cannot get
the dam to hold back
water, figure out a way
to seal it to the floor of
the bin. Remember, real
dams have foundations
below the floor of the
river or stream.

Task 4 How will you test your model?
It helps to go back to the original
problem you are trying to solve.
Sometimes it helps to test with a
small amount of water. *Be sure to
figure out how to get water out of
your model before you add any.*
Add a chart to your notebook to
record ratings for different designs.

Paula Schoeff et al.

DAM DESIGN CHALLENGE

Name: _____   Design Team: _____

Our dam is called:

_____

Now it is time to begin thinking like an engineer! Use the following blocks as you work through the problem like an Engineer. You will need four pieces of paper. Put the pages together and fold them in half, like a book. Give it a title, then turn the page and begin. Each step of the design process should take up an entire page.

Page 2: Define the Problem – Write it out in your own words

The teams are challenged to build an embankment dam which can hold back four liters of water. The site must have a sand and/or gravel bed. The dam must have at least one outlet which can open and shut to let water through.

Page 3: Learn – Brainstorm possible solutions

What type of dam will you be building?	Where is the water coming from? Where will most of the pressure be coming from?
Where should the outlet go?	Should we test with the outlet open or closed? Will it make a difference?

DAM DESIGN CHALLENGE

Page 4: Learn – Research, List Materials, and Identify the Next Steps

What will be the best shape for your dam? Explain why you will be using this shape.	How tall should the dam be to hold 4 liters of water? Explain why it needs to be this tall.
What materials will you be using? Explain why these are the best materials for the job.	Make a list of the steps you will follow to build your dam. Be sure to assign a job to everyone on the team.

Page 5: Plan – Draw a sketch before you build your dam

After answering the questions in your booklet, make a sketch with your ideas.

After drawing your sketch, meet with your team to make sure there isn't anything anyone wants to change or add.

Remember – label EVERYTHING – list the materials for each part, the size of each part (using metric is extra points, but using standard measurement is fine too), and, of course, the name of each part.

Finally, make a supply list. Be thorough, you don't want to have to hold up the process while you wait on shipping to get your parts in.

Page 6: Try - Build your dam using your sketch as a model. Test it

Start with the sand and/or gravel. Is it working like you hoped it would? What works, what doesn't. Write about what happened in your booklet. Add a chart to your notebook to record ratings for different designs that you try.

DAM DESIGN CHALLENGE

Page 7: Test and Decide

You have your reflections, review them and talk with the team if you need to make changes – brainstorm with the team and write about these changes. Explain what you will do and why this will be an improvement in your STEM research notebook. After your model begins to work, it is time to make improvements. Hint: if you cannot get the dam to hold back the water, figure out a way to seal it to the floor of the bin. Remember, real dams have foundations below the floor of the river or streams.

Page 8: Share – Engineers know they must share their ideas and use feedback

At least one member from another team must sign the back of your book. They will write two sentences which provide feedback to make your dam better.

     The sentences should look something like this:

This dam uses a good design. I like ...

_____

This dam could be better if ...

_____

STUDENT HANDOUT

WRITING THE OREO WAY TEMPLATE

Name _____

Opinion	Give your opinion.
Reason	State the reason for having this opinion.
Example	Give an example that supports your opinion.
Reason	State a second reason for having this opinion.
Example	Give a second example that supports your opinion.
Opinion	Restate your opinion.

Paula Schoeff et al.

ENERGY INFOGRAPHIC RUBRIC, PAGE 1 OF 2

Name:_____ Team Name:_____

	Exceeds Expectation (5)	Meets Expectation (4)	Approaching Expectation (3)	Needs Improvement (1–2)	Score
Observations	• Observations are accurate & complete. • Interpretations are based on experiences and observations.	• Observations are accurate & complete. • Interpretations are based only on lab observations.	• Observations are accurate, but miss important details. • Lab did not inform interpretation.	• Observations are not accurate or are missing • Missing or inaccurate interpretations available.	
Predictions	• Clearly understands what will happen. • Explains predictions and identifies reasoning with confidence.	• Understands what will happen. • Explains predictions with gaps in understanding.	• Grasps the idea of what will happen. • Predictions are explained with gaps in understanding.	• No predictions made. • Reasoning for predictions is not clear.	
Drawings and sketches	• Drawings are detailed. • Detailed labels and descriptions. • Labels reflect appropriate vocabulary.	• Drawings contain several details. • All the important labels and descriptions are present. • Labels reflect a growing vocabulary.	• Drawings contain some details. • Labels drawing, but leaves out some important details. • Labels include few science terms.	• Drawing is not detailed. • Labels are incorrect, confusing, or non-technical. • No science terms used.	

ENERGY INFOGRAPHIC RUBRIC, PAGE 2 OF 2

	Exceeds Expectation (5)	Meets Expectation (4)	Approaching Expectation (3)	Needs Improvement (1–2)	Score
Data and Results	• Tables/graphs are neat and clearly labeled. • Tables/graphs are accurate and used effectively. • Data is shown with the best method so that patterns/trends can be seen.	• Tables/graphs are labeled. • Tables/graphs are all accurate, but not helpful. • Some data is show with the best method so that some patterns can be seen.	• Tables/graphs are mislabeled. • Tables/graphs are inaccurate and difficult to interpret. • Data is unclear so that it is not possible to make clear predictions.	• Much of the data is not recorded on the tables/graphs. • It is not possible to use the tables/graphs to find a pattern. • Incorrect corrections are made due to bad data.	
Total Score					
Comments:					

OPINION WRITING RUBRIC

Name: _____   Total Score: _____

	Exceeds Expectation 4	Approaching Expectation 2	Meets Expectation 3	Needs Improvement 1	Score
Question	Question is posed and demonstrates insight beyond expectations	Question is posed but may not be clear	Question is posed	Question is not posed	
Answer to Question	Question is answered in a clear, logical way.	Question is partially answered.	Question is restated and answered in a logical way.	Question is not answered correctly.	
Explanation	Explanation is thorough and argument is very convincing.	Explanation is weak and confusing.	Explanation is based on evidence.	Explanation is not complete and no evidence is provided.	
Organization	Work is neat and organized and is above expectations!	Work is unorganized.	Work is organized and demonstrates proficiency.	Work is not neat and clear.	
Mechanics and Spelling	No spelling or grammar errors.	Some spelling and grammar errors.	Few spelling and grammar errors.	Many spelling and grammar errors.	
Total Score					
Comments:					

ENERGY INFOGRAPHIC RUBRIC, PAGE 1 OF 2

Name:_____ Team Name:_____

	Exceeds Expectations 3	Meets Expectation 2	Needs Improvement 1	Score
Topic	The topic is specific and is intended to inform or convince the viewer.	The topic may be a bit too broad to allow the viewer to understand the main points.	The topic is hard to determine and needs to be more specific.	
Content – Accuracy	At least four accurate facts are used and represent the topic well.	At least three accurate facts are used and represent the topic adequately.	Two or fewer accurate facts are used but do not represent the topic well.	
Visual Effects	The colors chosen and the shape, size arrangement of graphics are eye-catching and contribute to the topic.	The colors chosen and the shape, size arrangement of graphics are varied, but do not add to the topic.	The colors chosen and the shape, size arrangement of graphics are distracting and hide the message.	
Objects	The objects used are repeated to support the data and to make it easier for the viewer to understand the content.	Some objects used are repeated, but there are not enough repeated elements to make it easy to understand.	Too many different types of objects were used and it makes it difficult to understand the content.	
Data Representation	The formats for data make it easy for the viewer to understand the information.	The format for data show the information, but some of the information is lost or difficult to understand.	The presentation is confusing; a different format should have been used for the data.	

ENERGY INFOGRAPHIC RUBRIC, PAGE 2 OF 2

	Exceeds Expectations 3	Meets Expectation 2	Needs Improvement 1	Score
Design	The layout is neat, clear and visually appealing.	The layout is appealing, but is a bit messy.	The layout is messy and poorly designed.	
Mechanics	Spelling and grammar are perfect!	There are a few spelling and grammar errors.	There are numerous spelling and grammar errors.	
Total Score				
Comments:				

Lesson Plan 4:
Big Changes for Millside Corners
Design Challenge

In this lesson teams address the module challenge by creating and presenting a proposal for the Empire Creek Hydroelectric Plant and Dam. Teams will each create a sketch and fine-tune their proposals and will prepare and participate in the Millside Corners Debate at the annual Fossil Fair.

ESSENTIAL QUESTIONS

- What elements need to be added to convert Davis Mill into a hydroelectric power plant?

- What elements can be modified on the Empire Reservoir dam to improve its efficiency?

- How do environmental factors influence decisions about the size, shape, and materials used in construction of a dam?

- What evidence is available to support converting Davis Mill and the Empire Reservoir dam into a hydroelectric plant?

- What other options are available for producing this area's electricity in a sustainable way?

ESTABLISHED GOALS AND OBJECTIVES

At the conclusion of this lesson, students will be able to do the following:

- Use the EDP to develop a model of a hydroelectric power plant and dam which maximizes the efficiency of water pressure

- Effectively utilize shapes, materials, and measurements to create a model of a hydropower system

- Describe important details of a hydroelectric power plant and dam in a written proposal

- Develop an argument to support an opinion using evidence

- Participate in a debate using findings from their research

TIME REQUIRED

7 days (approximately 45 minutes each day; see Table 3.9–3.10, pp. XX–XX)

Paula Schoeff et al.

MATERIALS

Required Materials for Lesson 4

- STEM Research Notebooks

- Computer with Internet access for viewing slideshow

- Handouts and resources (attached at the end of Lesson 4)

  - Big Changes for Millside Corners Design Challenge student handout

  - Building an Argument student handout

- Rubrics

  - Written Proposal Rubric

  - Model and Sketch Rubric

  - Debate Rubric

Additional Materials for Big Changes For Millside Corners Design Challenge (for each team of 3–4 students)

- large sheet of paper or poster board (22″ × 28″)

- colored pencils

- ruler

- fine-tipped black marker

- a variety of craft materials as needed to build the models: modeling clay, cardboard, poster board, craft sticks, dowel rods, colored construction paper, straws, foam pipe insulation.

- 4 sheets of unlined white printer paper per team (for booklets)

SAFETY NOTES

1. Remind students that personal protective equipment (safety glasses or goggles, aprons, and gloves) must be worn during the setup, hands-on, and takedown segments of activities.

2. Students should use caution when handling scissors as the sharp points and blades can cut or puncture skin.

3. Tell students to be careful when handling containers. Cut plastic may have sharp edges, which can cut or puncture skin. Plastic can break and cut skin.

CONTENT STANDARDS AND KEY VOCABULARY

Table 4.11 lists the content standards from the *NGSS, CCSS,* and the Framework for 21st Century Learning that this lesson addresses, and Table 4.12 presents the key vocabulary. Vocabulary terms are provided for both teacher and student use. Teachers may choose to introduce some or all of the terms to students.

Table 4.11 Content Standards Addressed in STEM Road Map Module Lesson 4

NEXT GENERATION SCIENCE STANDARDS

PERFORMANCE OBJECTIVES
- 4-ESS3-1. Obtain and combine information to describe that energy and fuels are derived from natural resources and their uses affect the environment.
- 4-PS3-2. Make observations to provide evidence that energy can be transferred from place to place by sound, light, heat, and electrical currents.
- 4-PS3–4. Apply scientific ideas to design, test, and refine a device that converts energy from one form to another.

DISCIPLINARY CORE IDEAS

ESS3.A: Natural Resources
- Energy and fuels that humans use are derived from natural sources, and their use affects the environment in multiple ways. Some resources are renewable over time, and others are not.

PS3.A: Definitions of Energy
- Energy can be moved from place to place by mobbing objects or through sound, light, or electric currents.

PS3.B: Conservation of Energy and Energy Transfer
- Energy is present whenever there are moving objects, sound, light, or heat. When objects collide, energy can be transferred from one object to another, thereby changing their motion. In such collisions, some energy is typically also transferred to the surrounding air; as a result, the air gets heated and sound is produced.
- Energy can also be transferred from place to place by electric currents, which can then be used locally to produce motion, sound, heat, or light. The currents may have been produced to being with by transforming the energy of motion into electrical energy.

PS3.D: Energy in Chemical Processes and Everyday Life
- The expression "produce energy" typically refers to the conservation of stored energy into a desired form for practical use.

CROSSCUTTING CONCEPTS

Cause and Effect
- Cause and effect relationships are routinely identified and used to explain change.

Energy and Matter
- Energy can be transferred in various ways and between objects.

Systems and System Models
- A system can be described in terms of its components and their interactions.

Table 4.11 (*continued*)

SCIENCE AND ENGINEERING PRACTICES

Asking Questions and Defining Problems
- Ask questions that can be investigated and predict reasonable outcomes based on patterns such as cause and effect relationships.

Developing and Using Models
- Develop a model to describe phenomena.
- Use a model to test interactions concerning the functioning of a natural system.

Planning and Carrying Out Investigations
- Make observations to produce data to serve as the basis for evidence for an explanation of a phenomenon or test a design solution.

Constructing Explanations and Designing Solutions
- Identify the evidence that supports particular points in an explanation.
- Use evidence (e.g., measurements, observations, patterns) to construct an explanation.
- Generate and compare multiple solutions to a problem based on how well they meet the criteria and constraints of the design solution.
- Apply scientific ideas to solve design problems.

Obtaining, Evaluating, and Communicating Information
- Obtain and combine information from books and other reliable media to explain phenomena.

COMMON CORE STATE STANDARDS FOR MATHEMATICS
MATHEMATICAL PRACTICES
- 4.MP1. Make sense of problems and persevere in solving them.
- 4.MP2. Reason abstractly and quantitatively.
- 4.MP3. Construct viable arguments and critique the reasoning of others.
- 4.MP4. Model with mathematics.
- 4.MP5. Use appropriate tools strategically.
- 4.MP6. Attend to precision.

MATHEMATICAL CONTENT
- 4.MD.A.2. Use the four operations to solve word problems involving distances, intervals of time, liquid volumes, masses of objects, and money, including problems involving simple fractions or decimals, and problems that require expressing measurements given in a larger unit in terms of a smaller unit. Represent measurement quantities using diagrams such as number line diagrams that feature a measurement scale.
- 4.MD.B.4. Make a line plot to display a data set of measurements in fractions of a unit (1/2, 1/4, 1/8). Solve problems involving addition and subtraction of fractions by using information presented in line plots.
- 4.MD.C.5. Recognize angles as geometric shapes that are formed wherever two rays share a common endpoint, and understand concepts of angle measurement.

COMMON CORE STATE STANDARDS FOR ENGLISH LANGUAGE ARTS
READING STANDARDS
- RI.4.1. Refer to details and examples in a text when explaining what the text says explicitly and when drawing inferences from the text.

Table 4.11 (*continued*)

- RI.4.2. Determine the main idea of a text and explain how it is supported by key details, summarize the text.
- RI.4.3. Explain events, procedures, ideas, or concepts in a historical, scientific or technical text, including what happened and why, based on specific information in the text.
- RI.4.4. Determine the meaning of general academic and domain-specific words or phrases in a text relevant to a grade 4 topic or subject area.
- RI.4.6. Compare and contrast a firsthand and secondhand account of the same event or topic; describe the differences in focus and the information provided.
- RI.4.7. Interpret information presented visually, orally, or quantitatively (e.g., in charts, graphs, diagrams, time lines, animations, or interactive elements on Web pages) and explain how the information contributes to an understanding of the text in which it appears.
- RI.4.9. Integrate information from two texts on the same topic in order to write or speak about the subject knowledgeably.

WRITING STANDARDS
- W.4.2. Write informative/explanatory texts to examine a topic and convey ideas and information clearly.
- W.4.6. With some guidance and support from adults, use technology, including the Internet, to produce and publish writing as well as to interact and collaborate with others; demonstrate sufficient command of keyboarding skills to type a minimum of one page in a single sitting.
- W.4.7. Conduct short research projects that build knowledge through investigation of different aspects of a topic.
- W.4.8. Recall relevant information from experiences or gather relevant information from print and digital sources; take notes and categorize information, and provide a list of sources.
- W.4.9. Draw evidence from literary or informational texts to support analysis, reflection, and research.

SPEAKING AND LISTENING STANDARDS
- SL.4.1. Engage effectively in a range of collaborative discussions (one-on-one, in groups, and teacher-led) with diverse partners on *grade 4 topics and texts*, building on others' ideas and expressing their own clearly.
- SL.4.4. Report on a topic or text, tell a story, or recount an experience in an organized manner, using appropriate facts and relevant, descriptive details to support main ideas or themes; speak clearly at an understandable pace.
- SL.4.5. Add audio recordings and visual displays to presentations when appropriate to enhance the development of main ideas or themes.

FRAMEWORK FOR 21ST CENTURY LEARNING
- Interdisciplinary Themes (financial, economic, & business literacy; environmental literacy)
- Learning and Innovation Skills
- Information, Media & Technology Skills
- Life and Career Skills

Table 4.12 Key Vocabulary in Lesson 4

Key Vocabulary	Definition
argument	an important point of debate or controversy
controversy	a heated discussion of something about which there is a difference of opinion
debate	when two speakers or teams challenge one another in a formal contest of argument
issue	an important point of debate or controversy
model	a smaller representation of something very large or a large representation of something very small that shows the important components of the original
moderator	the manager of a public discussion or debate
prototype	a rough model used to refine a final design
rebuttal	in a debate, an argument presented to counter the other side's position

TEACHER BACKGROUND INFORMATION

In the Introductory/Engagement activity of this lesson, you will review the alternatives confronting the townspeople in the Big Changes for Millside Corners Design Challenge, including the following:

- Build a bigger dam

- Retrofit the existing unit at Davis Mill

- Build a run-of-river system

- Something else … or none of the above.

Dam Design and Hydropower

For additional background information on dam design and hydropower, please refer to these resources:

- Dam design and general hydropower facts: https://water.usgs.gov/edu/wuhy.html; https://www.energy.gov/eere/water/hydropower-basics

- Run-of-river dam illustration: https://www.youtube.com/watch?v=162o0aMHUfs

- An animation showing the operation of a hydro turbine: https://www.youtube.com/watch?v=Lx6UfiEU3Q0

Big Changes for Millside Corners Design Challenge

In this lesson, the previous weeks' work is capped off by the design project that addresses the module's primary challenge. Student teams will each build a three-dimensional model that will demonstrate how to optimize the efficiency of a dam using the dam models they built earlier in the module.

Each team should review the hydropower alternatives and determine the system that will best fit the town's needs. It is not unlikely that multiple teams will choose the same option. The engineering students from Buckeye University favored a run-of-river style solution since it provided the power station with the same power as a larger dam, while necessitating few changes to the dam itself. Figure 4.23 shows the plan the Buckeye University students proposed (this image is included in the Big Changes for Millside Corners slideshow at www.routledge. com/9781032618074).

Figure 4.23 Buckeye University plan to triple the power of the dam

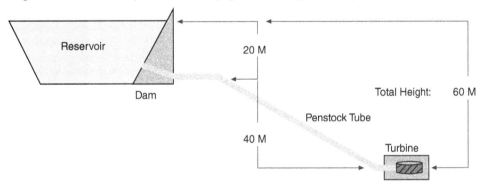

Photo credit: Pandaia Projects LLC. See Internet Resources section for link to licensing information.

Classroom Debates

By simplifying debate rules for the elementary classroom and taking advantage of the excitement of a debate format, students can experience the value of the research, critical thinking, and presentation skills that are part of the formal debate process. The simplified format used in this lesson is as follows:

1. Opening and Position Statements (12 minutes): Each speaker for each side of the issue opens with a different argument.

   - 6-minute Opening and Position Statement – Speaker/Team 1

   - 6-minute Opening Position Statement – Speaker/Team 2

- Each team must present its entire argument inside the 6-minute time limit.

- Each team should consider different aspects of their argument: economic, philosophical, historical, etc.

- Numbers, facts, and expert quotes/opinions are an important part of the argument.

1. Timeout – 2 minutes

   - During timeout, the team puts together its defense to refute the opponent's concerns.

2. Rebuttal – 8 minutes

   - 4-minute Rebuttal– Speaker/Team 1

   - 4-minute Rebuttal – Speaker/Team 2

3. Timeout – 1 minute

4. Crossfire – Moderator Lead Questions (4 minutes)

   - The moderator(s) now have an opportunity to ask a question that both teams will respond to (2 minutes each).

   - The questions should be focused on the Empire Creek and Davis Mill problem.

   - The moderator(s) should not be biased in his or her questions or tone.

5. Timeout – 2 minutes

6. Closing Summaries (4 minutes)

   - 2-minute Closing Summary – Team1

   - 2-minute Closing Summary –Team2

     - This is the last attempt to convince the audience, so speakers should take notes of the most compelling arguments are most likely to counter the arguments of their opponents and refocus on the central issue.

     - Choose one issue which matters the most and use this issue to frame the final parting shot.

The following are recommended ground rules for classroom debates:

- Opponents may never interrupt one another, but the moderator may stop one person from taking too much time to answer the question.

- Opponents should speak respectfully to one another and to the moderators

- During the opening statements someone on the team should take notes of the opponent's arguments.

- New content (e.g., additional facts, statistics, or expert advice) can be brought up during the rebuttal stage.

COMMON MISCONCEPTIONS

In this lesson, students are synthesizing their learning from previous lessons and therefore no new misconceptions are introduced. It will, however, be helpful to review the misconceptions introduced in Lessons 1–3 and be alert to ongoing misconceptions such as those presented.

PREPARATION FOR LESSON 4

Review the Teacher Background Information provided, assemble the materials for the lesson, make copies of the student handouts, and preview the slideshow recommended in the Learning Plan Components section below.

During the Introductory/Engagement portion of the lesson, you should be prepared to reread the challenge narrative, Students' Scoop on Millside Corners, from Lesson 1 and focus on the following details:

- Millside Corners' history as an agricultural center

- The role of Davis Mill in early electrification efforts

- Millside Corners' tourist industry

- The hydropower study done by Buckeye University students

- The new opportunities for clean energy opened up by the study

To prepare for the class debate, be prepared to have students position their desks facing each other at the front of the room. Prepare a poster with ground rules for debating (see Teacher Background, p. XX for suggestions). Select student (s) to serve as the moderator(s) before you begin. Make sure that the moderators are aware that this is an important role since it the moderators' job to make sure all important issues are represented, to keep the debate conflict-free, and track the time for each person's/team's presentations. Part of the moderator's role will

also be to come up with engaging questions to pose during the crossfire part of the debate.

LEARNING PLAN COMPONENTS
Introductory Activity/Engagement

Connection to the Challenge: Begin each day of this lesson by directing students' attention to the module challenge, Big Changes for Millside Corners Design Challenge. Hold a brief class discussion each day of how students' learning in the previous days' lessons contributed to their ability to complete the challenge. You may wish to create a class list of key ideas on chart paper.

Science Class and Mathematics, ELA, and Social Studies Connections: Tell students that in this lesson they will address the module challenge, Big Changes for Millside Corners Design Challenge. Review the current state of hydropower in Millside Corners and some of the alternatives using the Google slideshow, Big Changes for Millside Corners at www.routledge.com/9781032618074. A discussion guide is provided below.

Big Changes for Millside Corners Discussion Guide

Remind students that Millside Corners is a little town in southern Ohio located on Empire Creek, just downstream from the Empire Creek reservoir. The town is small, but it is a popular destination for artists and musicians and has several festivals in the summer, including the Fossil Fair. Remind students that at one time the town got its electricity from Davis Mill, a converted grain mill on Empire Creek. Now the town's power comes from a gigantic coal powered plant one hundred miles away. Davis Mill still has a generator driven by the water wheel, but it is used only to power the mill's main building.

Hold a class discussion about the implications of introducing hydropower to Millside Corners, asking the following questions:

- Do you think it would be fun to live in a town like Millside Corners? What do you like about the town? What do you not like?

- Consider the saying "If it ain't broke, don't fix it." Can you think of a time when a change was made to something that was not "broke" and the result was a big improvement? How about the opposite – can you think of a change was made to something that was not "broke" and the result was much worse?

- If you had super powers and could easily convert Millside Corners from coal power to hydropower, would you do it? Why or why not?

Point out to students that a civil engineering class at Buckeye University recently conducted a study of the dam at the reservoir. They determined that there was enough water flow to supply more than enough power for Millside Corners and the area around it. At a town meeting, the university students offered ideas about harnessing water power to supply clean energy. Ask students to name the alternatives they have learned about:

- Some people think that Millside Corners should build a larger dam with turbines located at the base of the dam. A higher dam means more water pressure and more power.

- Some people think Millside Corners should modernize the generator in Davis Mill by improving the dam's efficiency with modern components. This would involve replacing the water wheel with a turbine.

- Some people think Davis Mill should be replaced by a power station. This would involve connecting the dam to the new power station at Davis Mill. This would utilize the same dam but provide more power.

- Some people think that everything should stay the same, leaving Davis Mill as a tourist attraction and getting power from the coal powered plant.

Since many people in Millside Corners are interested in moving to renewable energy, tell students that the town has asked for their help in making the best choice. Each team will use the EDP to plan a solution and build a model of a hydropower system that can provide renewable energy for the town and the area around it. Teams can use one of the plans listed above or propose another plan.

Activity/Exploration

Science Class and Mathematics, ELA, and Social Studies Connection: Review with students that as part of the Big Changes for Millside Corners Design Challenge their teams will each develop a three-dimensional model that will demonstrate how to optimize the efficiency of a dam. The model may be combined with sketches or posters to communicate the overall design of the system.

Big Changes for Millside Design Challenge

Remind students that in previous weeks they explored various aspects of a hydro-power system, including the following:

- how to increase power by increasing vertical distance from reservoir surface to turbine.

- that turbine design affects performance and efficiency.

- that minimizing friction reduces energy loss.

Student teams each built working prototypes for a turbine (the Water Wheel Design Challenge in Lesson 2) and a dam (the Dam Design Challenge in Lesson 3) that can be used in students' solutions to the module challenge. Teams may wish to modify their designs or create new designs for the challenge.

Hold a discussion about models, asking students the following questions:

- Have you ever seen models of machines or buildings in a school, museum, or science center? What different kinds of models are there? *Possible answers might include: 3D model, blueprint or plans, animation or simulation, artist's sketch or rendering.*

- Engineers and architects often build models of their designs when trying to convince people to make a change. Why do they do that?

- How are models useful?

- What are the limitations of models for understanding something?

- Engineers and scientists use their knowledge and experiments to build complicated machines and devices. Is the question "Will it work?" the only question that engineers should ask before designing and building something? What other questions should they ask?

Distribute the Big Changes for Millside Corners Design Challenge student handout to each student. Introduce the following guidelines to students for their models:

- Student teams should choose from one of the hydropower alternatives (see Introductory/Engagement section, p. XX) or a new solution.

- Teams should build a model illustrating the main points of their system design including:

  - Dam design

  - Power plant design

  - Water path to the power plant – either within the dam or through a penstock tube leading down river

- At least part of the model should be three-dimensional; preferably the section where performance improvements are implemented. The model can be fully three-dimensional or a combination of posters, sketches, and three-dimensional objects.

- If a run-of-river or pumped storage alternative is selected, model components should be arranged at different heights to convey an idea of increased water pressure by increased vertical distance.

- Because of the size of a typical hydropower system, the main components of the system (dam, power plant, and penstock) need not be shown on the same scale.

- If designs are modified in the Try stage, the original sketches should be revised to match the prototype.

- Teams should use the EDP to create their model using the following steps:

  - *Define*: decide what factors affecting their design decisions.

  - *Learn*: Brainstorm: identify the best hydropower alternative, conduct research as necessary, and decide on a design.

  - *Plan*: Research and design the system.

  - *Try*: Build the model.

  - *Test and Decide:* Collaborate with at least one other team for feedback and make improvements based on the feedback.

Explanation

Science Class and Mathematics Connection: In addition to the models, each student should create a written proposal for their solutions. These proposals should include a rationale for the selected alternative as well as a description of how the solution would be implemented.

ELA and Social Studies Connections: Students will participate in the Millside Corners Debate. Introduce the debate by holding a discussion about debates, asking students the following questions:

- Have you ever seen a debate on TV or in a video? What are some of your observations about the debate?

- How could a public debate help the people of Millside Corners make a decision about the hydropower question?

- Sometimes people who want change say they are doing it "for the children." What do you think they mean by this?

Tell students that they will debate the question "Should Millside Corners convert Davis Mill into a hydroelectric power plant?" Student teams should prepare a strong argument for the side of the debate they have been assigned, using evidence that they

hope will persuade others to support their view. Make a recommendation that the team have a minimum of three strong ideas supported with evidence, but remind them that having more will provide an opportunity to bring in new information later in the debate (during the second round and crossfire sections).

Have each team to elect a team captain. Using their research, have each team plan their arguments. They will need to decide which points are most important so they can cover those first. They will also need to imagine what the opponents' arguments will be so they can devise a strategy for reinforcing their own claims. Use the debate format outlined in the Teacher Background section (p. XX). Tell students that their team is not required to use all of the time designated, but they will be required to stop at the allotted time. Team members are prohibited from speaking to the audience or opposing team members except at times when the moderator deems it will be beneficial. Introduce the ground rules provided in the Teacher Background section (p. XX).

Distribute the Building an Argument student handout to each student and review with students. Have student teams prepare their arguments, encouraging students to incorporate their learning from the module and permitting them to use their models and information from their proposals. Each student should complete a Building an Argument handout using ideas the team agrees on.

Elaboration/Application of Knowledge

Science Class and Mathematics, ELA, and Social Studies Connection: Hold the class debate about the question "Should Millside Corners convert Davis Mill into a hydroelectric power plant?"

Evaluation/Assessment

Students may be assessed on the following performance tasks and other measures listed.

Performance Tasks

- Big Changes for Millside Corners models
- Big Changes for Millside Corners written proposals
- Hydropower Debate
- Building an Argument

Other Measures

- Teacher observations

- STEM Research Notebook entries

- Student participation in teams

INTERNET RESOURCES

- Dam design and general hydropower facts: https://water.usgs.gov/edu/wuhy.html; https://www.energy.gov/eere/water/hydropower-basics

- Run-of-river system video: www.youtu.be/dXBYbRCx0JQ

- Animation of hydro turbine: www.youtu.be/Lx6UfiEU3Q0

- Big Changes for Millside Corners slideshow: www.routledge.com/9781032618074

Image Link
Student Model: https://www.flickr.com/photos/10485077@N06/5151787057/
Owner: edenpictures License: Attribution 2.0 Generic (CC BY 2.0)

4   Paula Schoeff et al.

BIG CHANGES FOR MILLSIDE CORNERS DESIGN CHALLENGE

Name: _____ Design Team: _____

Now it is time to begin thinking like an engineer! You will make a booklet with your plans. Use the blocks below as you work through the problem like an engineer. You will need four pieces of paper. Put the pages together and fold them in half, like a book. Give your booklet a title. You should create a section of the book for each task listed below and work through the design process.

Task 1: Define the Problem (Pages 1 and 2 of your booklet)

Description What problem have the townspeople asked you to solve?	Project Strong Points What benefits can a hydropower project bring to Millside Corners?
Environment How will a hydropower project affect the environment around the reservoir, dam, and Empire creek?	Other Things to Consider What other limits might be important? Cost of the project, effect on tourism, etc.?

BIG CHANGES FOR MILLSIDE CORNERS DESIGN CHALLENGE

Task 2: Learn – Brainstorm possible solutions (pages 3 and 4 of your booklet)

Build a Bigger Dam How can we make the dam big enough to give us the power we need?	Modernize Davis Mill What can we do to get more power from the generator at the mill?
Replace Davis Mill with a Hydropower Plant How can we keep our small dam and still generate the power we need?	Other Hydropower Ideas What hydropower systems could let us keep the mill and the dam as they are?

Task 3: Plan– Research, list materials, and identify the next steps (pages 5 and 6 of your booklet)

Dam Design – Research It! What changes do we need to make at the dam? (Cite your resources.)	Whole System – Research It! How do we connect the parts of our system?
Power Plant – Research It? How do we make our turbines efficient in the power plant? (Cite resources.)	Environment – Research It! How can our hydropower system be friendly to the environment? (Cite resources.)

4

Paula Schoeff et al.

BIG CHANGES FOR MILLSIDE CORNERS DESIGN CHALLENGE

Task 4: Try – Follow your plan and build a model (pages 7 and 8 of your booklet)

After filling out the form, make sketches with your ideas: dam, power plant, and system layout. After drawing your sketches, meet with your team to get more ideas that you might want to change or add. Once your design is perfect, decide how you will make your model. You can reuse your turbine from Lesson 2 for the power plant. You can reuse or remake your dam from Lesson 3. Arrange the dam and power plant as you envision them in your system. Show how the dam and power plant will be connected.

Remember – label EVERYTHING – list the materials for each part, the size of each part (using metric is extra points, but using standard measurement is fine to), and, of course, the name of each part.

Task 5: Test and Decide – Engineers know they must share their ideas and use feedback (pages 9 and 10 of your booklet).

At least one member of another team must sign your booklet. They will write two sentences that provide feedback to make your slide better. The sentences should look something like this:

This system uses a good design. I like ...

_____

This system could be better if ...

_____

NATIONAL SCIENCE TEACHING ASSOCIATION

BUILDING AN ARGUMENT

Evidence to back up my reasons

MAIN IDEA... *This is what I think...*

COUNTER ARGUMENTS

1. MY REASONS

You COULD argue...

2.

3.

Paula Schoeff et al.

WRITTEN PROPOSAL RUBRIC

Name: _____ Team: _____ Score _____

Points	Content	Mechanics
25	• Meets or exceeds all requirements. • Name and title are provided. • Clear rationale for choice of hydropower alternative. • Describes the hydropower system and layout clearly. • Considered power output and provides evidence. • Environment and tourism are discussed objectively while effectively expressing passionate arguments for proposal.	• 3–5 well-written paragraphs with topic sentences and conclusions that are easy to follow. • No spelling errors or grammar errors. • Proposal is neatly written.
20	• Meets all requirements. • Name and title is provided • Clear description of the hydropower system. • Considered power output and made reasonable choice. • Environment and tourism are discussed objectively with persuasive reasoning.	• 3–5 well written paragraphs that are easy to follow. • No spelling errors and 2–3 errors in grammar, capitalization, or punctuation. • Proposal is neatly written.
10	• Name and/or title is provided • Sentences are not in order and difficult to follow • Describes the system but lacks clarity • Considers power output • Either the environment or tourism are addressed effectively when providing reasoning for proposal.	• 3–5 paragraphs, but sentences are formed with several ideas joined together and are difficult to follow. • No more than two spelling, and five grammar, capitalization, or punctuation errors. • Proposal is not neatly written.
5	• No name or title is provided. • Did not describe the system. • Did not consider power output. • Did not consider environment or the impact on tourism.	• Is not 3 paragraphs or is more than 5 paragraphs long and is difficult to follow because of sentence structure. • Many spelling and grammar, capitalization, and punctuation errors. • Proposal is not neatly written.

MODEL AND SKETCH RUBRIC, PAGE 1 OF 2

Name _____ Team _____ Score _____

Points	Content	Mechanics
25	• Model and sketches have detailed notes about measurements (suggested angle, length and width of units). • The shape of the dam and other elements of the system are considered and effectively increases strength and functionality of the system. • Material is noted where needed on the model. • Model and sketches are self-explanatory. • The new design is unique and very creative.	• Everything for the model is identified and described on the sketches. • Sketched portions are colored to indicate materials used and neat. • A key for scale and a color-code key is provided for the materials.
20	• Model and sketches have notes about measurements (suggested angle, length and width of unit). • The shape of the dam is considered and effectively increases strength and functionality of the structure. • Material is noted sometimes on the model. • Model and sketches need some explanation. • The new design for the dam or mill is different than the previous versions.	• Most items are identified and described on the sketches. • Sketched portions are colored to indicate materials used and are neat. • A key for scale and a color-code key is provided for the materials.
10	• Model and sketches have some notes about measurements (suggested angle, length and width of unit). • Some shapes of the system are considered in the sketch to increase strength and functionality. • Material notes are random or inconsistent. • Model and sketches are not clear. • The new design for the dam or mill is similar to the previous versions.	• Title and descriptions are provided near the model. • Sketched portions are colored or are neat, but not both. • Modeled portion not is labeled. • A key for scale or a color-code key is provided for the materials.

MODEL AND SKETCH RUBRIC, PAGE 2 OF 2

Points	Content	Mechanics
5	• Model and sketches do not have notes about measurements (suggested angle, length and width of unit). • Shape research is not reflected in the sketches. • No indication of materials in model or sketches. • Model and sketches seems unrelated. • The new design for the dam or mill shows no improvement over previous versions.	• No title or description is provided. • Sketched portions are not colored or neat. • Modeled portion not recognizable in sketches. • A key for scale nor color-coding is provided.

DEBATE RUBRIC, PAGE 1 OF 2

Pro Team Name _____ Con Team Name_____

A scale of 1 to 5 will be used to grade each team. 1 = poor and 5 = excellent.		PRO Team	CON Team
OVERALL PERFORMANCE			
1.	The team was well prepared for the debate.		
2.	The team worked well as a team.		
3.	The team remained respectful throughout the debate.		
4.	The team seemed confident, energetic, and passionate about their topic.		
OPENING STATEMENT			
5.	The opening statement was well organized and effective.		
6.	The team presented plenty of evidence to defend its position.		
7.	The presentation was creative and interesting.		
8.	The arguments were presented in a clear and logical manner.		
9.	The time was managed well.		
REBUTTAL			
10.	The rebuttal addressed the concerns that arose in an effective manner.		
11.	The team's response was focused and clear.		
12.	The team was able to target weaknesses in the opponents argument and strategically address these weaknesses.		
13.	The team appeared to know both sides of the debate well.		

DEBATE RUBRIC, PAGE 2 OF 2

1 = poor and 5 = excellent.	PRO Team	CON Team
RESPONSE TO QUESTIONS		
14. The team provided informed answers to the questions.		
15. The team used practical evidence when answering the questions.		
16. The team did not get flustered during the questioning.		
17. The responses were clear and persuasive.		
CLOSING STATEMENT		
18. The final statement summarized the arguments in a persuasive way.		
19. The position statement on the board was consistently reinforced.		
20. The final statement sounded convincing and gained your support.		

REFERENCES

Koehler, C., Bloom, M. A., & Milner A. R. (2015). The STEM Road Map for grades K–2. In *STEM Road Map: A framework for integrated STEM education*, ed.

TRANSFORMING LEARNING WITH HYDROPOWER EFFICIENCY AND THE *STEM ROAD MAP CURRICULUM SERIES*

Carla C. Johnson

This chapter serves as a conclusion to the Hydropower Efficiency integrated STEM curriculum module, but it is just the beginning of the transformation of your classroom that is possible through use of the *STEM Road Map Curriculum Series*. In this book, many key resources have been provided to make learning meaningful for your students through integration of science, technology, engineering, and mathematics, as well as social studies and English language arts, into powerful problem- and project-based instruction. First, the Hydropower Efficiency curriculum is grounded in the latest theory of learning for students in grade 4 specifically. Second, as your students work through this module, they engage in using the engineering design process (EDP) and build prototypes like engineers and STEM professionals in the real world. Third, students acquire important knowledge and skills grounded in national academic standards in mathematics, English language arts, science, and 21st-century skills that will enable their learning to be deeper, retained longer, and applied throughout, illustrating the critical connections within and across disciplines. Finally, authentic formative assessments, including strategies for differentiation and addressing misconceptions, are embedded within the curriculum activities.

The Hydropower Efficiency curriculum in the Sustainable Systems STEM Road Map theme can be used in single-content classrooms (e.g., mathematics) where there is only one teacher or expanded to include multiple teachers and content areas across classrooms. Through the exploration of the Hydropower Efficiency lesson plans,

Carla C. Johnson

students engage in a real-world STEM problem on the first day of instruction and gather necessary knowledge and skills along the way in the context of solving the problem.

The other topics in the *STEM Road Map Curriculum Series* are designed in a similar manner, and NSTA Press and Routledge have published additional volumes in this series for this and other grade levels, and have plans to publish more.

For an up-to-date list of volumes in the series, please visit: https://www.routledge.com/STEM-Road-Map-Curriculum-Series/book-series/SRM (for titles co-published by Routledge and NSTA Press), or https://www.nsta.org/book-series/stem-road-map-curriculum (for titles published by NSTA Press).

If you are interested in professional development opportunities focused on the STEM Road Map specifically or integrated STEM or STEM programs and schools overall, contact the lead editor of this project, Dr. Carla C. Johnson, Professor of Science Education at NC State University. Someone from the team will be in touch to design a program that will meet your individual, school, or district needs.

APPENDIX

CONTENT STANDARDS ADDRESSED IN THIS MODULE

NEXT GENERATION SCIENCE STANDARDS

Table A.1 (p. 222) lists the science and engineering practices, disciplinary core ideas, and crosscutting concepts this module addresses. The supported performance expectations are as follows:

- 4-ESS3-1. Obtain and combine information to describe that energy and fuels are derived from natural resources and their uses affect the environment.

- 4-PS3-2. Make observations to provide evidence that energy can be transferred from place to place by sound, light, heat, and electrical currents.

- 4-PS3-4. Apply scientific ideas to design, test, and refine a device that converts energy from one form to another.

Table A.1 Next Generation Science Standards (NGSS)

Science and Engineering Practices
ASKING QUESTIONS AND DEFINING PROBLEMS • Ask questions that can be investigated and predict reasonable outcomes based on patterns such as cause and effect relationships. DEVELOPING AND USING MODELS • Develop a model to describe phenomena. • Use a model to test interactions concerning the functioning of a natural system. PLANNING AND CARRYING OUT INVESTIGATIONS • Make observations to produce data to serve as the basis for evidence for an explanation of a phenomenon or test a design solution. CONSTRUCTING EXPLANATIONS AND DESIGNING SOLUTIONS • Identify the evidence that supports particular points in an explanation. • Use evidence (e.g., measurements, observations, patterns) to construct an explanation. • Generate and compare multiple solutions to a problem based on how well they meet the criteria and constraints of the design solution. • Apply scientific ideas to solve design problems. OBTAINING, EVALUATING, AND COMMUNICATING INFORMATION • Obtain and combine information from books and other reliable media to explain phenomena.
Disciplinary Core Ideas
ESS3.A: NATURAL RESOURCES • Energy and fuels that humans use are derived from natural sources, and their use affects the environment in multiple ways. Some resources are renewable over time, and others are not. PS3.A: DEFINITIONS OF ENERGY • Energy can be moved from place to place by mobbing objects or through sound, light, or electric currents. PS3.B: CONSERVATION OF ENERGY AND ENERGY TRANSFER • Energy is present whenever there are moving objects, sound, light, or heat. When objects collide, energy can be transferred from one object to another, thereby changing their motion. In such collisions, some energy is typically also transferred to the surrounding air; as a result, the air gets heated and sound is produced. • Energy can also be transferred from place to place by electric currents, which can then be used locally to produce motion, sound, heat, or light. The currents may have been produced by transforming the energy of motion into electrical energy. PS3.D: ENERGY IN CHEMICAL PROCESSES AND EVERYDAY LIFE • The expression "produce energy" typically refers to the conservation of stored energy into a desired form for practical use.
Crosscutting Concepts
CAUSE AND EFFECT • Cause and effect relationships are routinely identified and used to explain change. ENERGY AND MATTER • Energy can be transferred in various ways and between objects. SYSTEMS AND SYSTEM MODELS • A system can be described in terms of its components and their interactions.

Source: NGSS Lead States. (2013). *Next Generation Science Standards: For states, by states.* Washington, DC: National Academies Press. *www.nextgenscience.org/next-generation-science-standards.*

Table A.2 Common Core Mathematics and English/Language Arts (ELA) Standards

Common Core State Mathematics Standards	Common Core State English Language Arts (ELA)
MATHEMATICAL PRACTICES • MP1. Make sense of problems and persevere in solving them. • MP2. Reason abstractly and quantitatively. • MP3. Construct viable arguments and critique the reasoning of others. • MP4. Model with mathematics. • MP5. Use appropriate tools strategically. • MP6. Attend to precision. MATHEMATICAL CONTENT • 4.MD.A.2. Use the four operations to solve word problems involving distances, intervals of time, liquid volumes, masses of objects, and money, including problems involving simple fractions or decimals, and problems that require expressing measurements given in a larger unit in terms of a smaller unit. Represent measurement quantities using diagrams such as number line diagrams that feature a measurement scale. • 4.MD.A.3. Apply the area and perimeter formulas for rectangles in real world and mathematical problems. • 4.MD.B.4. Make a line plot to display a data set of measurements in fractions of a unit (1/2, 1/4, 1/8). Solve problems involving addition and subtraction of fractions by using information presented in line plots. • 4.MD.C.5. Recognize angles as geometric shapes that are formed wherever two rays share a common endpoint, and understand concepts of angle measurement.	READING STANDARDS • RI.4.1. Refer to details and examples in a text when explaining what the text says explicitly and when drawing inferences from the text. • RI.4.2. Determine the main idea of a text and explain how it is supported by key details, summarize the text. • RI.4.3. Explain events, procedures, ideas, or concepts in a historical, scientific, or technical text, including what happened and why, based on specific information in the text. • RI.4.4. Determine the meaning of general academic and domain-specific words or phrases in a text relevant to a grade 4 topic or subject area. • RI.4.6. Compare and contrast a firsthand and secondhand account of the same event or topic; describe the differences in focus and the information provided. • RI.4.7. Interpret information presented visually, orally, or quantitatively (e.g., in charts, graphs, diagrams, time lines, animations, or interactive elements on Web pages) and explain how the information contributes to an understanding of the text in which it appears. • RI.4.9. Integrate information from two texts on the same topic in order to write or speak about the subject knowledgeably. WRITING STANDARDS • W.4.1. Write opinion pieces on topics or texts, supporting a point of view with reasons and information. • W.4.2. Write informative/explanatory texts to examine a topic and convey ideas and information clearly. • W.4.6. With some guidance and support from adults, use technology, including the Internet, to produce and publish writing as well as to interact and collaborate with others; demonstrate sufficient command of keyboarding skills to type a minimum of one page in a single sitting. • W.4.7. Conduct short research projects that build knowledge through investigation of different aspects of a topic. • W.4.8. Recall relevant information from experiences or gather relevant information from print and digital sources; take notes and categorize information, and provide a list of sources.

Table A.2 (*continued*)

Common Core State Mathematics Standards	Common Core State English Language Arts (ELA)
	• W.4.9. Draw evidence from literary or informational texts to support analysis, reflection, and research. SPEAKING AND LISTENING STANDARDS • SL.4.1. Engage effectively in a range of collaborative discussions (one-on-one, in groups, and teacher-led) with diverse partners on *grade 4 topics and texts*, building on others" ideas and expressing their own clearly. • SL.4.4. Report on a topic or text, tell a story, or recount an experience in an organized manner, using appropriate facts and relevant, descriptive details to support main ideas or themes; speak clearly at an understandable pace. • SL.4.5. Add audio recordings and visual displays to presentations when appropriate to enhance the development of main ideas or themes.

Source: National Governors Association Center for Best Practices and Council of Chief State School Officers (NGAC and CCSSO). (2010). *Common core state standards.* Washington, DC: NGAC and CCSSO.

Table A.3 21st Century Skills from the Framework for 21st Century Learning

21st Century Skills	Learning Skills & Technology Tools	Teaching Strategies	Evidence of Success
Interdisciplinary Themes	• Global Awareness • Economic, Business, and Entrepreneurial Literacy • Health Literacy • Environmental Literacy	• Facilitate student use of the engineering design process (EDP) to create hydropower system models. • Support student research to help them understand the implications of efficiency and environmental impacts of various renewable energy resources.	• Students demonstrate an understanding of the EDP and use it successfully to create a model hydropower system. • Students discuss, in blogs, videos, or podcasts; in a written proposal; and in a debate, the advantages and disadvantages of a hydropower system.
Learning and Innovation Skills	• Creativity & Innovation • Critical Thinking & Problem Solving • Communication & Collaboration	• Introduce the EDP as a problem solving framework. • Facilitate critical thinking and problem solving skills through the design and building of hydropower system models. • Provide examples of blogs, podcasts, video clips, debates, and other means of making persuasive arguments.	• Students demonstrate an understanding of the EDP through teamwork to design hydropower system models. • Students demonstrate creativity and innovation, critical thinking and problem solving, communication, and collaboration as they plan, build, and test hydropower system models.

Table A.3 (*continued*)

21st Century Skills	Learning Skills & Technology Tools	Teaching Strategies	Evidence of Success
			• Students demonstrate creativity and innovation, critical thinking, problem solving, communication, and collaboration as they participate in a class debate about hydropower.
Information, Media and Technology Skills	• Information Literacy • Media Literacy • Information Communication and Technology Literacy	• Engage students in guided practice through the use of developmentally appropriate books, videos, and websites to advance their knowledge. • Facilitate student use of technology to conduct research to gain understanding of alternative power sources and to use simulations to better understand hydropower. • Facilitate student use of technology to share experiences and knowledge in blogs, podcasts, or videos.	• Students acquire and use deeper content knowledge via information gained from media and technology as they create hydropower system models and consider the implications of hydropower.
Life and Career Skills	• Flexibility and Adaptability • Initiative and Self-Direction • Social and Cross-Cultural Skills • Productivity and Accountability • Leadership and Responsibility	• Facilitate student collaborative group work to foster life and career skills.	• Throughout this module, students collaborate to conduct research, complete design projects, plan for a debate, and create hydropower system models.

Source: Partnership for 21st Century Learning. (2015). Framework for 21st Century Learning. *www.p21.org/our-work/p21-framework.*

Table A.4 English Language Development Standards Addressed in STEM Road Map Module

English Language Development Standards: Grades 3–5 (WIDA, 2020)
ELD Standard 1: Social and Instructional Language   Multilingual learners narrate, inform, explain, and argue.
ELD Standard 2: Language for Language Arts   Multilingual learners will construct and interpret language arts narratives and arguments and construct and interpret informational texts.
ELD Standard 3: Language for Mathematics   Multilingual learners will interpret and construct mathematical explanations and arguments.
ELD Standard 4: Language for Science   Multilingual learners will interpret and construct scientific explanations and arguments.
ELD Standard 5: Language for Social Studies   Multilingual learners will interpret and construct social studies arguments.

Source: WIDA. (2020). *WIDA English language development standards framework, 2020 edition: Kindergarten–grade 12.* Board of Regents of the University of Wisconsin System. *https://wida.wisc.edu/sites/default/files/resource/WIDA-ELD-Standards-Framework-2020.pdf.*

INDEX

Page numbers in italic indicate a figure and page numbers in bold indicate a table on the corresponding page

For Product Safety Concerns and Information please contact our EU
representative GPSR@taylorandfrancis.com
Taylor & Francis Verlag GmbH, Kaufingerstraße 24, 80331 München, Germany

www.ingramcontent.com/pod-product-compliance
Ingram Content Group UK Ltd.
Pitfield, Milton Keynes, MK11 3LW, UK
UKHW030829080625
459435UK00017B/594